"NANCY DREW, WHAT ARE YOU DOING?" BESS
DEMANDED SUSPICIOUSLY.

The Secret of Red Gate Farm.   Page 153.

"WHAT IS THE MATTER?" CRIED NANCY HURRYING
TO HER.

The Secret of Red Gate Farm.

"HOW MUCH DO I OWE YOU?" HE DEMANDED OF
THE ATTENDANT.

The Secret of Red Gate Farm. **Page 64.**

SNIGGS SUCCEEDED IN HOLDING BACK GEORGE AND
BESS, BUT NANCY WRIGGLED FROM HIS GRASP.

The Secret of Red Gate Farm. Frontispiece (Page 185.)

NANCY DREW MYSTERY STORIES

THE SECRET OF RED GATE FARM

BY

CAROLYN KEENE

AUTHOR OF "THE SECRET OF THE OLD CLOCK,"
"THE HIDDEN STAIRCASE," ETC.

ILLUSTRATED BY
RUSSELL H. TANDY

WITH AN INTRODUCTION BY
AMANDA CROSS

FACSIMILE EDITION

BEDFORD, MASSACHUSETTS
APPLEWOOD BOOKS

For further information about these editions, please write: Applewood Books, Box 365, Bedford, MA 01730.

LIBRARY OF CONGRESS CATALOGING-IN-PUBLICATION DATA
Keene, Carolyn.

The Secret of Red Gate Farm / by Carolyn Keene; illustrated by Russell H. Tandy; with an introduction by Amanda Cross.—Facsimile ed.

p.   cm.   —(Nancy Drew mystery stories)

Summary: Nancy becomes suspicious of a secret society and is drawn to investigate.

ISBN 1-55709-160-9

[1. Mystery and detective stories.]   I. Tandy, Russell H., ill.   II. Title.   III. Series: Keene, Carolyn. Nancy Drew mystery stories.

PZ7.K23Sd   1994

[Fic]—dc20   94-41449
                                          CIP
                                          AC

10 9 8 7 6 5

HOPING TO GO TO THE RESCUE

By

AMANDA CROSS

AUTHOR OF

ELEVEN KATE FANSLER MYSTERIES

WHILE VERY YOUNG, I read the Nancy Drew books with a compulsion that shut out the rest of the world in a way no other book, however compelling, has managed to do since. What I most admired about Nancy Drew was the way she found people who needed to be rescued and always managed to help them. I, like many girls, entertained secret fantasies of rescuing people in need, people whose lives I could make happy. Of course, girls were not supposed to have the power or the initiative to rescue anyone, and, in fact, they did not. Girls were persuaded, indeed almost compelled, to adopt what was considered properly "feminine" behavior: passivity, gentle receptiveness, and the patience for a man to arrive and offer a destiny. Yet, for some girls, the urge to step in, to intervene, to alter events and evoke possibilities was intense. All the other books we read and the movies we saw showed us that boys, and only boys, could alter the fortunes of grown human beings. Nancy Drew alone showed me that such a desire to go out and shake up events and people was not beyond imagining.

In the 1930s, when the original of *The Secret of Red Gate Farm* was written, in the years, that is, when I was just becoming an avid reader, the idea of a girl's venturing beyond the domestic sphere to rescue anyone was hardly thought of. Except by Nancy Drew.

Yet we dreamed of rescues: perhaps of arriving just in time to prevent a terrible miscarriage of justice; perhaps of finding someone in a difficult, even hopeless, situation, and saying to that person, "All will be well; I shall help you." We had such fantasies but, apart from Nancy Drew, little chance to read of them, unless we pretended to be the boys who were always the heroes of such rescue stories. We girls were always being told, in subtle and not so subtle ways, that we were there to be rescued, to wait for some man to come along; we were not there to do anything really interesting on our own.

Nancy Drew offered us a wonderful secret hope. From the very first of her adventures, *The Secret of the Old Clock*, in which she sets out to defeat the attempts of bad people to cheat good people of their rightful inheritance, Nancy Drew was the rescuer, the one who said, "This is not right and I intend to do something about it." Brave words, and how I longed to say them! That longing was somewhat assuaged by the fact that

Nancy Drew said them for me, and, what is more, went to the rescue and succeeded in her efforts in book after book.

Rescue was not, of course, the only thing that attracted us to the Nancy Drew books. We loved her independence. We admired her father, who thought everything she did was wise and intelligent. We noticed the absence of a mother—not sadly absent but somehow not there to keep Nancy Drew safely at home, to prevent her from rushing off in all directions. We loved her lack of attention to boys. We cheered her friend George, adored by all of us who hated how girls dressed up and acted prissy, and we happily tolerated her friend Bess, who liked dressing up and doing "feminine" things, but who nonetheless was willing to join in on all the adventures. Above all, I think, we loved that little blue roadster, which seemed to represent all the freedoms we, the avid followers of Nancy's adventures, did not enjoy.

And oh, how I wanted to be able to turn to a sad girl I met on a train (always supposing I would have been on a train alone with my friends and no grown-up, which was highly unlikely), as Nancy Drew does in *The Secret of Red Gate Farm*, when she meets Millie Burd, who faints right before Nancy's eyes. Nancy Drew takes her in charge, and suggests a way to solve her family's financial problems. Nancy Drew also captures, or at least helps the police to capture, a group of sinister criminals. This was the way one ought to be able to live.

On top of that, the police are always impressed by Nancy Drew, or, if they are not immediately impressed by *her*, then the very mention of her father's name does the trick. So Nancy Drew never has the trouble most young women have in getting important adults to listen to them. What is uphill work to most sixteen-year-olds—getting important people to pay attention to the vital information they have—is, for Nancy Drew, as easy as snapping her fingers.

There is another point that I found compelling when I was young, and still do: Nancy Drew does not consider that she must find a man to provide the center of her life. The idea never enters her mind, nor do her friends George and Bess discuss men much either. Since that was all most girls discussed in the long ago days when I read Nancy Drew, this was a fact that was especially important to me. I grew so tired of girls who sat around planning their weddings and gossiping about some cute boy or other. Boys were fun to play with, but if I had been honest I would have admitted, to myself and to others, that I would rather have been a boy than plan to marry one. Nancy Drew encouraged me to think about my ambitions and what I could make of my life as an individual human being, as a rational creature.

I spent my girlhood in New York City, skating

everywhere. Skates in those days had four metal wheels, one at each corner. They were extremely noisy going along, and skating over uneven sidewalks was bumpy. The skates didn't come with shoes attached; you put the skates onto your own shoes with a skate key that you wore around your neck after the skates were on tight. In this rather noisy, but I thought wonderfully adventurous fashion, I, an only, lonely, and largely independent child in a much safer city got about—a bit, just a bit, as Nancy did in her roadster.

Now, the funny part of all this is that it never occurred to me that Nancy Drew didn't live in a city as I did. I imagine that all her girl readers pictured her similarly in circumstances very much like their own. It was only a few years ago, when I was in Iowa City and met Mildred Wirt Benson, the author of these early, wonderful Nancy Drew books, that I learned that the Nancy Drew stories were in fact set in a small Iowa town. For me, and I daresay for many others, they were set exactly where I lived—unlikely as that might have been. But then, Nancy Drew's life was unlikely too, however eagerly we imagined ourselves leading it, and rescuing the unhappy people we could see about us every day.

Nancy Drew's being able to come to the rescue of those she felt needed her help has had a lasting effect on me. And when I, and I daresay many other women detective story writers, first dreamed about our detectives and what they would be like, I think that Nancy Drew's inclination and ability to rescue people was there in our minds. My detective, like so many women detectives—and unlike most American male detectives at any time—has also tried, though in a more complicated world than sixteen-year-olds face, to rescue those few people to whose aid she is able to come. Rescue, rather than revenge, personal anger, or the thrill of the hunt, is what has motivated my detective and, I suspect, most of the other followers of Nancy Drew. I grew up wanting my detective to rescue those badly in need of help and with nowhere else to turn. Nancy Drew showed me, long ago, that a woman could do it.

NANCY DREW MYSTERY STORIES

THE SECRET OF RED GATE FARM

BY

CAROLYN KEENE

AUTHOR OF "THE SECRET OF THE OLD CLOCK,"
"THE MYSTERY AT LILAC INN,"
"THE BUNGALOW MYSTERY," ETC.

ILLUSTRATED BY

RUSSELL H. TANDY

NEW YORK
GROSSET & DUNLAP
PUBLISHERS

Made in the United States of America

NANCY DREW
MYSTERY STORIES
By CAROLYN KEENE

12mo. Cloth. Illustrated.

THE SECRET OF THE OLD CLOCK

THE HIDDEN STAIRCASE

THE BUNGALOW MYSTERY

THE MYSTERY AT LILAC INN

THE SECRET AT SHADOW RANCH

THE SECRET OF RED GATE FARM

GROSSET & DUNLAP, PUBLISHERS, NEW YORK

The Secret of Red Gate Farm

CONTENTS

Contents

THE SECRET OF
RED GATE FARM

CHAPTER I

An Interesting Experience

"Hurry, girls. Hurry. Come on! We'll miss our train. We can't carry another package. Look at the time."

Nancy Drew glanced anxiously toward the department store clock as she endeavored to draw her friends, George Fayne and Bess Marvin, from a counter upon which an attractive assortment of novelty jewelry was displayed. The three girls had left River Heights early that morning and had spent several hours shopping in the nearby city. George and Bess had found it impossible to resist the many alluring bargains, and money had melted as if by magic.

"We have everything now except the perfume," Bess declared, consulting her shopping list.

"We must let it go," Nancy announced

firmly, steering her friends toward the door. "It's two-twenty-five now, and our train leaves the station in twenty minutes. It won't wait for us, and if we miss it, we'll be too late getting home."

"Oh, all right," Bess gave in reluctantly, "but I did want it."

"If we don't get out of this store pronto, you'll not have enough money left to buy your ticket home," George, her cousin, who was inclined to be blunt and decidedly boyish, declared. "Practice self-control the way I do."

"Self-control! Oh! Oh!" Bess retorted. "I suppose you call a new hat, two dresses, three pairs of stockings and a pocketbook self-control!"

"Girls, girls!" Nancy chided, "if we don't hurry——"

"All right," Bess laughed. "Elbow a path for us and we'll try to follow."

The girls hurried through the crowded store, but as their arms were laden with packages of all shapes and sizes, they had more than one near-casualty before they reached the street. Bess collided with a lady of generous proportions who glared balefully upon her. In her embarrassment, Bess dropped several of her bundles and caused a traffic jam in the aisle while she gathered them up.

"Thank goodness!" she breathed in relief as

they finally reached the street. "I feel lucky to get out of there alive!"

"You'll be more lucky if you don't have to walk home," George retorted. "I know a short cut to the station that will save us ten minutes. We better take it, and be sure of our time. Poor Nancy looks alarmed."

The side street which she indicated was narrow and dingy and the girls were not impressed with its appearance, yet time was so short that they felt they could not afford to be too particular. They followed George at a breakneck pace, and by the time they had covered three blocks were gasping for breath. Not until they were within sight of the railroad station did they dare slacken their speed.

"We still have a little over ten minutes," Bess reported, looking at her wrist watch. "Let's slow down before I drop right here on the street. I'm too plump to rush along like this."

"It's good for you," George muttered brutally.

The girls had reached the corner of the street, and Bess, whose attention had been attracted to a quaint Oriental shop, paused abruptly before the show window.

"I'm sure they must keep perfume here!" she cried. "Let's stop and get some."

"We haven't time," Nancy protested.

"Yes, we have. We're right in sight of the station, and it won't take but a minute to get it."

Without waiting for further advice, Bess, rash girl that she was, darted into the shop. There was nothing for Nancy and George to do but to follow her.

A dark-complexioned young woman of foreign appearance who wore a vivid Chinese costume and yet obviously was not a full-blooded Chinese woman, came forward. Her smile, as she led them toward the perfume counter was extremely forced, and she spoke with a distinct accent.

Upon entering the shop, the girls had instantly been impressed by the heavy odor of a perfume with which they were not familiar. Nancy thought that it must be a rare Oriental scent and George and Bess were of the same opinion.

"What is it?" they asked the clerk eagerly.

She did not respond, but instead removed a bottle from the shelf and handed it to Bess.

"This isn't the same thing!" she protested.

"It's a very lovely perfume," the woman said condescendingly.

"But I want an Oriental scent," Bess declared in irritation. "Really, we're in a hurry!"

Nancy and George, who were even more

eager to depart, had ventured to do a little investigating of their own. While Bess was remonstrating with the clerk, Nancy quickly located a bottle of perfume on the counter which appeared to give forth the same odor that had attracted their interest. She handed it to Bess for her consideration.

"Oh, you don't want that!" the young woman told them hastily.

"But I do!" Bess insisted. "It's so different. It's just what I want."

"The odor is much too heavy." The woman reached for another bottle on the counter. "Now this perfume——"

"I think I'll take the other bottle. How much is it?"

"It really isn't for sale. I purchase that particular scent for a special customer of mine."

"Well, can't you order more?" Nancy broke in. "Surely this special customer won't object if we purchase a little of it. How much is the bottle?"

"Three dollars," the woman answered petulantly.

The girls looked aghast at the announcement, and Bess turned away.

"I can't buy it," she whispered to the others. "If I do, I'll not have enough money left to get home."

The woman in charge of the shop overheard

the whispered remark, and Nancy, who chanced to be looking directly at her, noticed how relieved she seemed. She was assailed with an overwhelming desire to own the bottle of perfume, even if it was ridiculously high in price.

"Look here," she said to George and Bess. "Why not pool our resources? I can spare a dollar."

"So can I," George declared, rummaging in her purse.

The money was laid on the counter by the three girls.

The woman scowled, and for an instant Nancy thought that she intended to refuse to sell them the perfume. Then, with a shrug of her shoulders, she accepted the money.

"You'll not like the perfume," she warned, as she wrapped up the package.

The girls did not respond, but snatched up their purchase and rushed out of the shop.

"Three dollars for a tiny bottle of perfume!" George exclaimed when they were outside. "It's grand larceny! It will have to be mighty good to be worth that price."

Nancy had realized that the perfume was much too expensive, but the unwillingness of the young woman to part with it had stimulated her interest. Her bargain instinct told her that if the saleswoman was reluctant to part with it, then it must be well worth the money.

"I think she deliberately raised the price so we wouldn't buy," Nancy declared. "It probably was foolish to do it, but the scent is unusual. No one will have anything like it in River Heights."

"Why would she raise the price?" Bess questioned as they hurried on down the street. "You'd think she would want to sell the perfume."

"Yes," Nancy agreed with a troubled frown, "she acted rather queerly about it."

"Snippy," George added. "I didn't like her looks. She was too flashy or something."

The girls had forgotten the incident by the time they reached the station. A long line stood at the ticket window and the train came rumbling in before Nancy had purchased the tickets for River Heights. Bess and George, who had gathered up all the packages and rushed out to the tracks, were nearly frantic with anxiety when Nancy finally came running with the tickets. No sooner had the three scrambled aboard than the train began to move out of the station.

"That was a close shave!" George gasped. "Oh, what a day!"

The train was crowded, and the girls did not find any vacant seats until they came to the last car. They sat down near a pale, extremely thin young girl and arranged their packages, trying to make them appear as inconspicuous as possible.

George and Bess fell to discussing their many purchases, gloating in particular over the bottle of perfume. Even though the package was wrapped, it gave off a faint odor which was very pleasing.

Nancy leaned her head back against the cushion, and as she relaxed, studied the faces of the nearby passengers. She thought that the girl who occupied the seat just opposite looked very tired and ill.

"Why are you so quiet, Nancy?" Bess demanded suddenly.

"Just resting," Nancy returned.

She did not tell her friends that she had become interested in the nearby passenger, for George and Bess often teased her about her peculiar habit of scrutinizing strange faces. In truth, Nancy's friendly curiosity had involved her in more than one unusual adventure, as readers already acquainted with her know.

The ride to River Heights was only a short one, and in less than an hour the girls observed that they would soon approach their own station.

"We'd better gather our bundles," said George.

Just at that moment the conductor came

through the car calling, "River Heights." The pale young girl started nervously, and began to collect her parcels.

"She's getting off here, too," Nancy said in an undertone to her friends.

George and Bess nodded indifferently and adjusted their hats. They hastily gathered up the packages on the seat. George reached up to remove a hat bag from the overhead rack.

"Do be careful," Nancy warned, seeing that George was having difficulty in securing the parcel. "Let me get it."

She spoke too late. George had managed to get her fingers on a corner of the hat bag, but as she pulled, it slipped from her hand and fell to the floor with a loud crash.

"The perfume!" Bess cried in horror. "I put it into the hat bag so we wouldn't have so many packages to carry!"

"And look at my shoe!" Nancy exclaimed. "I'm drenched with the stuff!"

George snatched up the paper bag, one side of which was soaking wet, and rescued Bess's hat. It was too late to save any of the precious perfume. The bottle had shattered into bits.

"Three dollars gone to smash," George muttered. "I'm very sorry. I didn't know the perfume was in that bag."

"Even if we have lost the perfume, we still

have the odor," Nancy laughed. "I think I'll carry it for life! I don't know whether I like that idea or not."

Already the heavy odor had permeated the car, and passengers in nearby seats flung open the windows.

"I'm glad we're getting off at the next stop," Nancy murmured in an undertone. "Everyone is laughing at us."

"That perfume is certainly powerful stuff," George returned. "It's enough to make a fellow faint."

The girls had been so engrossed in trying to clean up the wreckage, that they had not once glanced toward the young woman who occupied the opposite seat. Now, as Nancy turned her head, she was startled to see that the girl had slumped down in a dejected heap.

"She's fainted!" Nancy cried, moving quickly across the aisle.

She shook the girl gently, but there was not the slightest response from the frail little individual.

"See if there is a doctor in the car!" she ordered Bess, who was standing helplessly by her side.

By this time others in the car were aware of what had happened, and were crowding about, asking unnecessary questions and doing nothing to assist. There did not appear to be a doctor on the train, but as Nancy chafed the girl's hands she was relieved to see that she began to show signs of recovering consciousness.

George quickly raised the window so that the cool, fresh air blew in upon the girl's face. Stretched out upon the seat, she looked deathly pale.

"Is there anything I can do?" George asked.

"Stay here while I get some water!" Nancy commanded. "She's coming around now. I think she'll be all right in a few minutes."

She hurried to the water cooler at the far end of the car. As she was trying to extract a paper cup from the slot machine, a man who had been standing in the vestibule came toward her. Nancy would not have noticed him, had he not suddenly paused beside her. He made a pretense of waiting his turn to get a drink, yet she realized by the intent look upon his face that something had startled him. He was deliberately studying her!

Like a flash it dawned upon Nancy what had startled the man. It was the perfume! She fairly reeked with it.

She was not prepared, however, for what came next.

The man edged closer to her, glanced quickly about to see that no one was in the immediate vicinity, and muttered in a guttural tone:

"Any word from the Chief?"

Nancy was taken by surprise. She had never seen the man before, for it would have been impossible to forget such a crude face. His steel-gray eyes bored straight into her. Nancy was momentarily confused, and could think of nothing to say.

The stranger saw at once that he had made a mistake.

"Excuse me, my error," he murmured as he turned quickly away, "but that perfume—never mind!"

CHAPTER II

A New Acquaintance

NANCY stared blankly after the stranger, and wondered what he could have meant. Evidently he had taken her for another person, but even so, his actions had been most peculiar. What message had he expected to receive from her? How strange that he should speak of the perfume as though it had been the cause of his mistake!

Had Nancy's mind not been occupied with a more important matter, she might have worried over the brief encounter. As it was, she dismissed it entirely, and quickly filling a paper cup with iced water, rushed back to where George and Bess were working over the girl who had fainted. Nancy was greatly relieved to see that she was sitting up, supported on either side by the two girls, and that she was not so white.

"Do you feel better now?" Nancy asked. "Here, drink this."

"Thank you," she murmured.

The girl accepted the cup with a grateful

13

smile, and drank the refreshing iced water.

"I feel much better now," she said quietly. "How silly of me to faint. It was very kind of you to bother with me."

"It must have been the perfume," George declared. "A little is all right but a whole bottle is enough to knock one over!"

"I'm sure it wasn't the perfume," the girl returned quickly. "I haven't felt well since I first boarded the train early this morning."

The train had slowed down as it approached the station, and Nancy and her friends realized that unless they wished to be carried past their destination, they must hurry.

"I'm afraid we must say goodbye," Nancy said reluctantly. "We get off at River Heights."

"River Heights!" The girl glanced anxiously out of the window. "Oh, dear, I get off here, too! I had no idea we were so close."

"We'll help you," Nancy promised. "Do you really feel well enough to walk?"

"Oh, yes, I'm all right now. I'm so sorry to have caused you all this trouble."

Nancy took the stranger's handbag, and George and Bess collected the miscellaneous packages. Kindly passengers supported the girl as she made her way down the aisle. She hesitated uncertainly as she stepped from the train.

"I'm not very familiar with River Heights," she said to Nancy. "Which direction should I go to get downtown?"

"Don't you think you should see a doctor first? Look here, you're in no condition to be walking about the street. Haven't you any friends here to meet you?"

The girl shook her head.

"Then you must come home with me," Nancy announced with decision. "I left my roadster parked here by the station.

The girl started to protest, but Nancy and the others urged her on and soon had her comfortably established in the blue car.

"I haven't even told you my name," she said as she sank wearily back against the cushions. "I'm Millie Burd. I live with my grandmother at Red Gate Farm. That's at Round Valley."

Nancy introduced her chums and mentioned her own name. George and Bess thought it rather odd that Millie did not recognize the name of Drew, for both Nancy and her father were famous in River Heights, each in a different way. Carson Drew was a noted criminal lawyer, and Nancy, though still a girl, had solved several mysteries.

She had always lived a self-reliant life, for her mother had died many years before, and the management of the household had fallen upon her capable shoulders. At an early age she had

interested herself in her father's practice, and
due to an unusual set of circumstances, had become involved in a mystery of her own.
Her experiences in this connection are recounted
in the first volume of this series, entitled: "The
Secret of the Old Clock."

After that, her reputation established, it was
only a short time before she was involved in
cases which baffled professional detectives.

Her most recent adventure had taken her to
a western ranch. With Bess Marvin and George
Fayne she had gone to Shadow Ranch expecting to have a pleasant summer outing. The
vacation had started out tamely enough, if one
may use that word to describe moonlight pic-
nics, encounters with mountain lions, and bat-
tles with bucking broncoes, but the end had
been a different matter.

In a lonely mountain cabin Nancy and her
friends found a child of mysterious parentage,
and in endeavoring to help her they came into
direct conflict with a queer old woman and her
unscrupulous brother. For a time Nancy feared
that the mystery must go unsolved, but in the
end she cleared it up, and in addition aided her
friend, Alice Regor, whose father had disappeared many years before. This story is related in the volume, "The Secret at Shadow
Ranch."

The vacation had been so exciting that Nancy

and her friends doubted that another could ever come up to it, yet as George expressed it, "they were on their toes for something thrilling to turn up." While that "something" had evaded them up to now, they had not given up hope.

Though Nancy had always been interested in deep mystery cases, she was by no means an overly serious young person. She had less dignity than Bess, who usually tried to do the proper thing at the proper moment, but considerably more dignity than George, noted for her topsy-turvy ways.

Nancy would not admit that she was pretty but agreed that her golden hair and blue eyes were her best assets.

"How nice it must be to live on a farm," Bess remarked enviously, "and Red Gate is such a pleasant-sounding name."

"Red Gate is a lovely place, too," Millie Burd declared feelingly. "I have lived there with my grandmother ever since I can remember. The farm isn't kept up as well as it should be, though."

"What a pity," Nancy replied, as she started the automobile and headed it toward the Drew residence in the better section of the city. "Can't you do anything about it?"

"We could if we had money," Millie returned quietly. "That's why I left home today. I thought I might find work here."

Nancy frowned thoughtfully. She had recently been talking to her father about this subject.

"River Heights isn't a very good place for that, I'm afraid. There are a great many people out of work here now."

"I came in response to a particular advertisement."

"That's different. I hope you find something."

"So do I," Millie smiled. "If I don't—well, grandmother may lose Red Gate."

"You're not trying to lift a mortgage or anything like that?" Nancy inquired lightly. She did not mean to be inquisitive.

Millie nodded soberly.

"We simply must raise the money to pay off the amount we borrowed or grandmother will lose the farm. She hasn't any way of earning money, so it's up to me."

"Surely no one would be mean enough to take your farm," Bess, who knew little of business, murmured sympathetically.

"Huh!" George grunted. "The world is full of tricksters who cheat widows and orphans!"

"Granny is a dear," Millie went on, "but she takes everyone's advice about money matters. When the land boom was on, folks told her she was foolish not to buy another farm and sell it at a high price. She thought she could assure

my future that way. Well, all at once values
crashed, and there she was with an extra farm
on her hands, and she couldn't meet the pay-
ments on it. The farm went back to the original owners, and Granny had to put a heavy
mortgage on Red Gate, too. Now she's nearly
frantic with worry, because if she loses Red
Gate Farm, we'll be penniless."

As Millie finished her little tale of woe, Nancy
turned the car into the driveway.

"You must all come in and have tea," she invited. "Perhaps we can think of a way to help
Millie."

The three girls followed Nancy into the
house, and as soon as they were established in
the living room, she slipped out into the kitchen
to tell Hannah, the housekeeper, to prepare
sandwiches.

"You must be nearly starved," she said to
Millie a moment later. "I know I am."

"I'm rather hungry," Millie confessed. "I
haven't had anything to eat since last night."

"What?" the girls demanded in chorus.

"It was my own fault," Millie said hastily.
"Grandmother wanted me to eat breakfast, but
I was so excited about getting this position,
that I couldn't think of food. There wasn't a
diner on the train, so even if I could have
spared the money, I would have had to go without food."

"Why, you poor thing," Nancy cried. "No wonder you fainted. I'm going to tell Hannah to fix you something hot."

She did not listen to Millie's protest but hurried again to the kitchen. In a few minutes the meal was ready. Millie ate heartily and Nancy and her friends made a pretense of doing the same, so that their guest would not feel embarrassed.

"I do feel better," Millie announced when she had finished. "It was so good of you to bring me here."

"Not at all," Nancy said kindly. "We'd like to help you if we could."

"Thank you, but everything will be all right if only I get this position I am after." Millie glanced anxiously at the mantel clock. "I am afraid I must be going now, or I'll be too late to make the call this afternoon. Perhaps you can tell me how to get to this address?"

She removed a folded scrap of newspaper from her purse and handed it to Nancy. The advertisement asked for an office girl, but it was the name at the bottom of the paragraph that held Nancy's attention.

"Why, this advertisement says Riverside Heights!" she exclaimed. "You should have stayed on the train until you came to the next station!"

CHAPTER III

Nancy Tries to Help

"Why, I thought Riverside Heights and River Heights were the same place!" Millie Burd exclaimed in distressed surprise. "How silly of me to make the mistake! I'm always doing things like that."

"Riverside is only a few miles away," Nancy explained, "and the names are confusing. They're very much alike. I can't understand why people who name towns are not more thoughtful."

"Oh, dear, I don't know what to do now," Millie said anxiously. "It's so late already, and if I don't apply for that position this afternoon, I'll probably lose my chance of getting it. And I must get it."

Nancy had taken a decided liking to the girl and wished to help her if she could. Not only was Millie half sick from lack of proper food, but she had worked herself up into a nervous state. Should she fail to secure the position she might have a complete breakdown.

"See here," Nancy said, "I can take you over

to Riverside Heights in the roadster. It will take us only about fifteen minutes and you'll still have time enough to apply for the position."

Millie's face brightened instantly, but she was reluctant to accept the favor.

"I've troubled you enough as it is."

"Nonsense! We'll get started right away!" Nancy turned to Bess and George. "Do you want to come with us?"

"I'm afraid I must hurry home," Bess returned. "Mother will be wondering what is keeping me."

George likewise declined the invitation, saying that she was tired.

The girls quickly gathered up their things and returned to the roadster which Nancy had left parked at the curbing. She dropped Bess and George at their own homes, and then took the highway leading to the next city.

"I do hope I get there in time," Millie said anxiously as they sped swiftly over the paved road. "The position will mean so much to me and Grandmother!"

Nancy made no response as she stepped harder upon the accelerator. She hoped that Millie would be successful in her search for work, but she was afraid that the girl was not the type to succeed in the business world. She lacked confidence and poise. As they drove along, Nancy tactfully drew her out concerning her experience, and was secretly alarmed to learn that Millie had never before applied for a position. She had taken a high school course in typewriting but that constituted her chief qualification.

"Until lately there was never any need for me to earn a living," Millie explained. "I have always helped Grandmother on the farm. We keep a hired man, but even at that a great deal of the work falls upon me." As she spoke, she glanced ruefully at her small hands which had been coarsened from hard work.

The girls soon reached the city, and Nancy had little trouble in locating the address mentioned in the advertisement. She did not like the particular section, but did not mention this to her companion.

"Here we are," she said cheerfully, stopping the roadster in front of a dingy-looking office building.

Millie made no move to get out of the car, but sat nervously pressing her hands together.

"I'm a terrible coward," she confessed. "I don't know what in the world to say when I go in."

"Just tell them everything you can do," Nancy encouraged, "and don't be afraid to lay it on thick, as they always make allowance for that anyway."

"I know I'll make a mess of it."

"Want me to go in with you?"

"If you only will!"

"I don't mind in the least," said Nancy, as she snapped off the ignition and carefully locked the car. They entered the building, and after some difficulty located room 305, which had been mentioned in the advertisement.

"There's no name on the door," Nancy observed in perplexity, "but it must be the place."

The girls scarcely knew whether to knock or to enter boldly, and finally decided upon the latter course. As they stepped into the reception room, Nancy noted instantly that it was dirty and dingy. She felt an impulse to turn and walk out, but for Millie's sake tried not to show that she was unfavorably impressed.

"It looks as though you have a good chance to get the position," she whispered encouragingly to her companion. "I don't see any office girl, so they probably haven't chosen one yet."

At that moment a man came out of the inner office and surveyed the girls with hostile inquiry. He was tall and wiry, with sharp, penetrating eyes and harsh features. His suit was of the latest cut, but bold in pattern and color. His necktie was gaudy.

"Well?" he demanded, coldly surveying the two girls.

Millie found sufficient courage to take the advertisement from her pocket.

"I—I saw this in the paper," she stammered. "I came to apply for the position."

Nancy fancied that the man looked relieved, but the expression was gone in an instant. His glance swept Millie critically and passed on to Nancy, where it lingered.

"You lookin' for the job, too?" he demanded.

Nancy shook her head.

"I'm merely here with Miss Burd."

The man glanced at Millie again and said with a shrug of his shoulders:

"Go on in the other room. I'll talk to you in a minute."

Millie cast Nancy a doubtful glance and obediently stepped into the inner office.

"Look here, girlie," the man addressed Nancy, "wouldn't you like that job? I could use a little chick like you."

"I'm not looking for work, thank you," she returned aloof.

The man was on the verge of making some retort when the telephone rang. He scowled and went over to the table to answer it. As he took down the receiver he glanced nervously back toward Nancy.

"Hello," he growled into the transmitter. "This is Al! Shoot!"

Nancy undoubtedly would not have paid the

slightest attention to the conversation, had it not seemed to her that the man's address was rather unbusinesslike, to say the least. She was further surprised when she saw him reach for a paper and pencil and begin to scribble down a long list of figures. This in itself would not have been so peculiar, had he not continued to eye her askance, as though he feared she might discover something.

For at least ten minutes he copied meaningless figures upon the paper. Nancy watched him curiously.

"O. K., Hank," he muttered just before he replaced the receiver on its hook. "You say you've found a girl? Fine! We can't be too careful in this business!"

By this time Nancy was asking herself in what business the firm was engaged. Certainly the office itself gave no clue, nor had the telephone conversation been illuminating. She realized that poor Millie's chance of securing work was slight indeed, particularly as the man had said something about having found another girl. In all truth, she could not feel especially regretful, for she felt that Millie would never enjoy working in such an office, or for such a man as this one appeared to be.

"I was just taking down some stock quotations," the man remarked in an off-hand manner, as he arose from the telephone, and came back to Nancy.

"This isn't an investment house, is it?" Nancy inquired.

"No, you wouldn't call it that exactly," he returned with an unpleasant smirk. "We run a manufacturing business."

"I see," Nancy murmured, though she really did not see at all. She could not resist asking, "What do you manufacture?"

The man pretended not to hear and moved on to the inner office where Millie was patiently waiting. In his haste to escape further questions, he forgot to pick up the sheet of paper with the numbers on it.

Nancy by nature was not prying, but she felt that all was not as it should be, and told herself that if Millie were to work in the office, it behooved her to discover, if she could, the sort of business which was being conducted.

Unable to resist the temptation, she tiptoed over to the telephone table and glanced at the sheet of figures. She could make nothing of it, for the numbers were strung out horizontally upon the page, thus:

00308 06420 23145, 06584, 30061.

"Stock quotations, like fun!" Nancy told herself. "Now why did he lie about it? He must have been afraid I'd discover something!"

Nancy was the true daughter of her father, and nothing intrigued her more than a mystery. As she studied the page of curious figures, it suddenly dawned upon her that it might be a message in code. Otherwise, how could one account for the commas and periods which were interspersed throughout the page?

Nancy cast a quick glance toward the inner office. The door was open but the man sat with his back toward her. She knew she dared not take the paper, for it would be missed at once. If only there were sufficient time to copy it!

With one eye on the inner office, Nancy snatched up a blank sheet of paper and frantically scribbled down the figures, taking care to keep them in their right order. She could hear Millie and her prospective employer talking loudly, and realized that the interview was soon coming to an unpleasant end. She must work fast!

"Furthermore, you're not the type of girl I want in my office," she heard the man say scornfully as he pushed back his chair and arose. "I want a girl with a little snap!"

Nancy had copied only half the page, but she dared spend no more time at it. She thrust the paper into her bag and slipped back into her chair just a moment before Millie and the man emerged from the inner room. Nancy was an excellent actress, and though her heart was beating madly, she managed to remain outwardly serene.

She saw the man who had called himself "Al" glance quickly toward the telephone table, and start. He rushed across the room and with a muttered exclamation snatched the paper up and thrust it into his pocket. He looked sharply at Nancy, but apparently was satisfied that she had not left her chair, for her calm expression gave no indication of what was passing through her mind.

"Let's get out of here," Millie murmured in a low tone. Nancy saw that she was struggling to keep back the tears.

"All right," she agreed quietly.

She, too, was eager to be away, but did not wish to give the appearance of haste. She arose leisurely and followed Millie out of the door, well aware that her actions were being critically watched.

CHAPTER IV

SUSPICION

"DON'T feel bad because you didn't get the position," Nancy said kindly to Millie as soon as they were outside. "You wouldn't have wanted it, I'm sure."

"That man was detestable!" Millie shuddered. "He was so rude."

"I think he had already made some arrangement to secure another girl. At least, I heard him say something to that effect over the telephone."

Nancy had decided to say nothing to Millie about the rest of the message, for she could not prove that her suspicions were just. Even if the message had been in code, the business might be a perfectly legitimate one. Millie would only be alarmed.

"I don't know what to do now," the girl murmured dejectedly. "I can't go back to Red Gate Farm. I must find work!"

"Why not come back home with me?" Nancy suggested as they paused beside the roadster. "I'll be glad to have you as my guest for the

night, and in the morning we can make some
plans about your getting back to Red Gate
Farm.''

Millie shook her head proudly.

''No, I shouldn't think of allowing you to
go to any more trouble. I have some money.
I can find a boarding house.''

Nancy saw that Millie was hopelessly discouraged, and accordingly felt reluctant to part
with her. She knew that what the girl needed
more than anything else was a good night's rest
and plenty of wholesome food. In vain she
tried to urge her to return to River Heights as
her guest, for at least a few hours.

''I intend to look for work early tomorrow
morning,'' Millie insisted. ''I think I'll have
more chance of finding it here than I should in
River Heights.''

''You're probably right,'' Nancy admitted.

''I'd take the first train back to Round Valley if it weren't for Grandmother,'' Millie confessed. ''I can't bear to disappoint her.''

Nancy saw by her watch that the hour was
late, and she was unwilling that her new friend
should walk the streets hunting for a boarding
house. She therefore proposed that they search
for a suitable place together. Millie accepted
the offer gratefully.

Even with the roadster, it was not an easy
task. Millie could not afford a high priced

place, and many of the rooms at which they looked were quite impossible. At last, however, they found a small boarding house on a quiet street, which was entirely satisfactory. Nancy waited until Millie was comfortably established before she said goodbye.

"I may be driving over this way tomorrow," she declared. "Perhaps I'll drop in to inquire what luck you have in job hunting."

"I wish you would," Millie invited. "I'll need someone to bolster up my courage."

"You mustn't let what happened today affect your nerve," Nancy said as she turned away. "That place we visited isn't a typical office by any means."

Nancy drove slowly toward River Heights, her mind occupied with the various events of the day. She was greatly interested in Millie and meant to keep an eye upon her.

"I don't know what will happen to her if she doesn't find work," she told herself. "It would be a shame if her grandmother loses Red Gate! I wish I could do something, but I can't even get her a position."

It was nearly dinner time when Nancy reached River Heights. She had no intention of stopping at the homes of either of her chums, but as she passed the Fayne home she saw George and her cousin on the lawn. She could not resist halting to tell them that Millie had been unsuccessful in her search for work.

"Now isn't that too bad," Bess murmured in disappointment. "She's such an unassuming little thing. I'd like to know her better."

"I'll go back tomorrow to see her," Nancy informed them. "Why don't you come along?"

"Let's!" George cried enthusiastically. "I like to go places with Nancy because we usually have some sort of adventure!"

Nancy smiled queerly at her friends, wondering what they would think if they knew all that had happened to her that day.

As Mrs. Fayne appeared on the front porch to summon her daughter to dinner, Nancy hastily said goodbye and drove on toward her own home. She had deliberately refrained from telling Bess and George about the strange telephone message which she had overhead.

"It's probably wiser to keep it to myself," she thought. "I'll ask Dad what he thinks about it tonight. I can trust him to keep the matter a secret."

Nancy had fallen into the habit of discussing puzzling problems with her father, for he never laughed at her ideas. Frequently he discussed his law cases with her, and had found her suggestions practical.

"You look tired, Nancy," Carson Drew observed as she entered the house by the rear door and tossed her hat into the first convenient chair. "Have a big day shopping? And what else did you and the girls do?"

"I can't remember when so much ever happened before in one day," she smiled in a weary way, as she dropped onto a comfortable lounge.

"I suppose I'll be getting the bills in a few days," her father remarked teasingly.

"I wasn't referring to the shopping alone," Nancy returned gravely as she sat down on the arm of her father's chair. "Other things happened—important things!"

Mr. Drew was not paying strict attention to what his daughter had said, for as she came near, he caught the odor of the strange perfume which still lingered upon her clothing.

"What have you been doing to yourself?"

"Don't be alarmed, Dad. It's only an Oriental perfume—a rather heavy dose, I'll admit. You'll appreciate it more when I tell you how I came to get it."

She then plunged into the story of how the perfume bottle had been broken, mentioning her encounter with the stranger on the train.

"What do you make of it?" she questioned.

Mr. Drew shook his head.

"Queer that he should ask you if you had received any word from the Chief! You're certain it was the perfume that attracted his attention?"

"I feel sure of it," Nancy announced firmly. "The man was polite enough but he looked like a gangster."

"H'm," Mr. Drew mused, "I can't say that I like the sound of this."

"Oh, I'll never see him again, Dad. He didn't pay any more attention to me as soon as he realized he had made a mistake. He didn't even get off at my station. I watched to see."

"I'm glad of that."

"I shouldn't have thought much about it, if it hadn't been that the girl in the store was so reluctant to sell the perfume in the first place," Nancy continued with a troubled frown. "Why do you suppose she cared who bought it?"

"It may have been her manner," Mr. Drew suggested. "I doubt that there is any connection between the incidents."

"Perhaps not," Nancy said slowly. She was not entirely convinced.

"You certainly did have an exciting day, but I don't believe there's any need to worry."

"Oh, I'm not worried—at least, not about that," Nancy smiled. "I haven't told you the most important part."

She then told her father about Millie Burd and described the office which they had visited together. She ended by showing him the page of figures which she had copied.

"This was only part of the message," she explained. "I didn't have time to copy the rest. Can you make anything of it?"

Carson Drew accepted the sheet of paper, and adjusting his glasses, studied it for some minutes in silence. Nancy watched his fingers as they moved back and forth over the page.

"I'm not an expert on codes," he said at last, "but I must say this certainly looks rather suspicious to me."

"I was hoping you could read it," Nancy commented in disappointment.

"I wish I could, but if this actually is a code, it is an especially complicated one. It would take me days to figure it out. Why don't you work on it yourself? I'd be glad to do it, only I have a very busy week ahead of me."

"I do intend to work on it," Nancy declared, "but I don't know anything about codes."

"I have a book on it that I'll be delighted to turn over to you," her father offered. "Not that it will help much, as every code that is worthy of the name is different. Still, they have some features in common. For instance, in any language certain words are repeated more frequently than others. If you can figure out a frequency table, and then look for certain numbers to appear more often than others, you may make some headway."

"And again, I may not," Nancy said doubtfully. "This sounds like a complicated business to me."

"It is complicated. Unless you are born with the right type of mind—analytical, I mean—codes are a closed book. This will be a good test of your brains."

"It may not be a code after all."

"That's possible," Mr. Drew agreed. "Of course, there is one way you could find out—turn it over to an expert on codes."

"Not until I've had a try at it myself," Nancy declared firmly. "However, there's one thing I wish you would do for me, Dad."

"What is that?"

"Try to find out what sort of business, if any, is being transacted at that office."

"I'll see what I can discover," Mr. Drew promised, "but you'll have to wait a few days at least. I can't look after anything until this Clifton case is off my hands."

The discussion closed as Hannah came into the living room to announce dinner. Nancy said no more about the matter during the meal.

Immediately after dinner Mr. Drew shut himself up in his study to work on his papers. Nancy tried to read a book, but she could not keep her mind upon the story. She kept thinking of Millie Burd.

"I almost wish she *had* secured that position this afternoon," Nancy thought regretfully.

"She might have found out what was wrong there! Oh, dear, why am I troubled with such an overwhelming curiosity?"

She flung aside her book and retired to her bedroom. Getting out the sheet of paper with the coded message, she studied the figures intently. She could make nothing of them.

"I'm sure the commas and periods are used as punctuation marks," she told herself, "but what the rest stands for is beyond me!"

After perhaps an hour of unsuccessful work she flung her pencil aside with an exclamation of disgust.

"It's plain to see I am one of those persons born without the right type of mind for codes!" she told herself as she jumped into bed. "Oh, well, I don't intend to lose any sleep over it!"

Little did she realize that codes were to cause her the loss of a great deal of sleep.

CHAPTER V

MILLIE BECOMES DISCOURAGED

THE next morning at breakfast Carson Drew handed his daughter a thin leather volume which he had unearthed from among the books and papers in his law library.

"This is the book I was telling you about," he declared, "but there isn't as much in it about codes as I thought. Still, you may be able to get a few pointers."

"I don't believe I'll make much headway," Nancy confessed, accepting the book gratefully. "I tried to figure out that message last night but I couldn't make head nor tail of it."

"Don't be discouraged so easily, Nancy. If it really is a coded message, I'm sure it is no simple affair. As soon as I get this Clifton case off my hands I may be able to help you. By the way, I'll not be home for luncheon to-day, and perhaps not for dinner."

"That suits me," Nancy returned, "because I thought I'd drive over to see Millie again to-day. She will probably need cheering up a bit. By the way, you don't happen to know of anyone who needs someone to work for him just now—I mean an office girl. Do you?"

Mr. Drew shook his head.

"I can't say that I do. Nearly everyone I know is turning away help these days. My guess is that your friend will have a difficult time finding a position."

"I'm afraid so," Nancy agreed with a sigh. "Millie is really cut out for a home girl. If it weren't that she wants to help her grandmother, I doubt that she would try to enter business."

After Carson Drew had taken his portfolio and departed for the office, Nancy busied herself about the house. As soon as she had attended to the usual morning duties, she settled herself in an easy chair and delved into the book which her father had given her.

She read with absorption, for the material was extremely interesting, but when she had finished she was no closer to the solution of her own problem, for, as her father had explained to her, the discussion on codes was more or less general.

"This is going to be worse than trying to figure out a Chinese crossword puzzle," she told herself. "Well, I'll have another try at it some other time."

The girls had planned to start for Riverside Heights early in the afternoon. As soon as the

luncheon dishes had been cleared away, Nancy
backed the blue roadster from the garage and
picked up Bess and George. By two-thirty they
had reached Millie's rooming house.

In response to Nancy's rap on the door, the
landlady came to admit the girls.

"Miss Burd's not in," she informed them.
"She left about two hours ago to see about a
job somewhere. She said to tell you she'd be
back before three o'clock."

"We arrived a little earlier than we had
expected," Nancy explained. "We don't mind
waiting for her."

The landlady invited them into the parlor,
but it was so dark and uninviting that the girls
preferred to wait outside in the roadster.

"It's a shame Millie has to live in a cheap
place like this," Nancy remarked. "Of course,
her room is clean and the neighborhood is re-
spectable, but Millie is the sort who needs
better surroundings."

"She has been accustomed to such an outdoor life, too," Bess added, "and even so, she
looks under-nourished and half sick. Goodness
only knows what she'll look like after she's
worked in the city for a few months."

"I do hope she finds something," George
said. "Perhaps that is what is keeping her
away so long."

Within fifteen minutes the girls caught sight

of Millie far up the street. She did not notice
the roadster parked at the curbing, and unaware that she was under observation, made
her way slowly toward the rooming house. She
looked very tired and her head drooped dejectedly.

"She didn't get it," George muttered. "Too
bad, isn't it?"

As Millie approached, Nancy hailed her. She
glanced up quickly and immediately mustered
a smile.

"What luck?" Bess questioned.

"None at all," Millie responded with an attempt at lightness. She came over to the car
and stood leaning against the door. "I tried
half a dozen places but I couldn't get a thing
to do. Still, I'm not discouraged. I'll find
something tomorrow, I'm sure."

In the face of such high courage the girls
could only utter words of encouragement,
though they were convinced that Millie did not
realize what she was up against.

"Wouldn't you like to take a little spin?"
Nancy invited.

"Indeed I would," Millie returned eagerly.
"It's so hot and stuffy in my room—" she
caught herself instantly. "Of course, it is
everywhere these days!"

Nancy selected a road which led out of the
city, and soon they were speeding along well

cultivated fields of corn and wheat. Gradually, Millie became more cheerful.

"I do love the country!" she declared, gazing wistfully toward a farm house which nestled among the rolling hills. "That place yonder looks something like Red Gate Farm, only it isn't half as nice. How I do wish you girls could visit me there sometime!"

"So do we!" Nancy returned. "Wouldn't it be great to roam wild on a farm?"

"I've always wanted to spend my vacation on a farm," Bess declared longingly. "Just imagine having cream an inch thick!"

"You're fat enough as it is," her cousin reminded her brutally. "I'll bet you couldn't tell a cow from a sheep!"

"I hope I learned that much at Shadow Ranch," Bess retorted.

"You wouldn't have any trouble at Red Gate," Millie smiled, "for we don't keep sheep and only a few cows. What money we make comes mostly from truck farming."

When the girls left Millie at her door three-quarters of an hour later they had the satisfaction of knowing that she was in a more cheerful frame of mind.

"We'll drive over again in a day or so," Nancy promised as they told her goodbye.

"I'll be looking for you," she answered.

It rained the following day and also the next.

On the third day Nancy and her chums kept their promise. They found Millie in very low spirits, indeed.

"I haven't been able to find work of any kind," she confessed unhappily. "Not even housework."

"Oh, Millie," Nancy protested quickly. "You're not strong enough for hard work!"

"I'd do anything to help out at home," Millie replied vehemently.

The girls were very much discouraged and troubled when finally they took their leave, for Millie, though admitting that her funds were running low, had refused to accept money from any of them.

"She can't hold out much longer," Nancy said thoughtfully as the girls were driving back to River Heights. "She's beginning to lose heart and her money is nearly gone."

"I feel terribly sorry for her," Bess declared, "but what can we do? She's too proud to accept money."

"I know," Nancy agreed.

She was so troubled about the girl that the following day she called upon a business acquaintance of her father in the hope that he might have something for her. He listened politely to all that she had to say, but when she had finished, shook his head regretfully.

"There are hundreds of girls just like her

out of work. I should like to help, but I am afraid I can't. However, I will take her name and if I hear of anything——"

After that, Nancy knew that it was only a matter of time before Millie must admit defeat and return to her home. So absorbed was she in the girl's future that the matter of the coded telephone message slipped into the background.

"I'm sick of it all," Millie admitted one day when Nancy had driven over to see her. The two girls were alone and she felt more free to speak her honest feelings. "I'd return to Red Gate in a minute if I could only find some means of raising money."

"Perhaps you can think of something," Nancy encouraged her. "Did you ever consider running a roadside inn?"

"We tried that once," Millie returned, "but our farm is too far from the main road. Grandmother inserted an advertisement in one of the city papers, asking for summer boarders. She hadn't heard anything from it when I left a week ago."

"Something may turn up yet."

"I doubt it," Millie sighed. "I guess I haven't much courage. I hadn't meant to tell Granny how things were going here, but a few days ago I was so blue that I sat down and wrote her everything."

"That was probably the best thing you could have done."

"Things can't go on as they have," Millie admitted gloomily. "I've been as economical as I could, but my money has simply flown!"

The conversation ended abruptly as there came a knock on the door. Millie arose to answer it.

"The mailman just left a letter for you," the landlady announced with a smile which was a trifle too sugary. "I thought you would be wantin' it so I brought it right up."

"Thank you," Millie responded, gratefully accepting the letter.

The landlady remained in the doorway, evidently hoping that Millie would open the letter in her presence. As she showed no signs of doing so, the woman reluctantly turned and went back down the stairs.

"She's the most prying thing," Millie declared. "I guess she is afraid I won't pay my next week's rent and is keeping tabs on me."

She glanced at the letter and noticed that the postmark bore the name of Round Valley.

"It's from Granny," she told Nancy. She turned the letter over in her hand and seemed reluctant to open it, obviously dreading what information it might contain.

At last, with a murmured apology, she ripped open the envelope. Her face lighted up.

"Grandmother wants me to come home right away," she reported. "Oh! Listen to this! Several persons responded to that ad she ran in the paper! They're arriving at Red Gate Farm next week, perhaps to spend the summer!"

"I'm so glad," Nancy said quickly. "Now you will not have to worry any more. You will really be better off at home."

"With so many guests coming there will be plenty of work for me to do, too! Not that I'll mind. I'm willing to work my fingers to the bone if only we can save Red Gate Farm!"

"Then everything is settled, isn't it?" Nancy asked in relief. "You'll go back to Round Valley tomorrow."

Millie nodded absently, her mind already far away. Suddenly a look of consternation passed over her face.

"Oh, I can't!" she cried.

"Why not?" Nancy questioned in surprise.

"I haven't enough money for train fare. When I pay my room rent for today I'll have less than two dollars left."

"If that's all that is troubling you, we'll soon settle that."

"Oh, but I don't like to take money," Millie protested. "I can write to Grandmother again and ask her to forward me enough to get home again."

"No need to do that," Nancy told her. "I have a better plan. I know a way to get you to Round Valley and it won't cost you a cent! Now don't ask me about the plan, because I haven't had time to work it out completely."

"You've gone to so much trouble for me already, you mustn't do another thing."

"I've enjoyed it, Millie, and if this plan that just occurred to me works out, you'll be able to repay me for any little thing that I may have done."

"If only I could!"

Nancy picked up her purse and arose to depart.

"You get your things packed and be ready to leave at ten o'clock tomorrow morning," she told Millie. "I don't know for certain how I'll get you to Red Gate Farm, but I'll find a way!"

CHAPTER VI

A Familiar Face

Nancy's plan was simple. If her father were willing, she proposed to drive Millie to Red Gate Farm in her own car. She estimated that the trip could be made in half a day.

Another idea had occurred to her, too. She recalled that Bess and George had both expressed a desire to spend a vacation on the farm, and since their parents were reasonably well-to-do there was no reason why this wish could not be carried into effect. Nancy accomplished a bit of mental arithmetic and reached the conclusion that three steady summer boarders who paid their bills regularly might do a great deal toward lifting the mortgage which hovered so menacingly over old Red Gate.

First of all, before broaching the subject to her chums, she was confronted with the necessity of securing her father's permission. That evening at dinner he gave her the desired opening.

"I'll be out of town for a week or so, Nancy," he told her regretfully. "Do you suppose you can get some of your friends to stay with you for that length of time?"

"I know of something better," Nancy informed him with a smile.

She then outlined her plan of aiding Millie Burd. As she had anticipated, her father agreed with her enthusiastically, and declared that if she wished to take George and Bess, she might drive his sedan, which was larger and more comfortable for a cross-country tour.

It was not as easy to convince Bess and George. They both wished to help Millie and agreed that a week or two in the country would be very pleasant, but there were various complications to be considered. If Bess went, it meant that she would lose out on a camping trip. George had planned to visit an aunt in Chicago, but admitted that the trip could be postponed.

"There's one thing about it," Bess laughed as she unwillingly agreed to give up the camping trip. "I've never been with Nancy yet that we didn't run into an adventure! Perhaps a trip to Red Gate will turn out to be exciting after all."

Bess and George experienced little difficulty in gaining their parents' consent. It was decided that on the following day the four girls should drive to Round Valley.

"There's one drawback to the plan," Nancy told her friends. "I haven't said anything to Millie about it. However, if there isn't room at the farm house, or her grandmother doesn't feel like keeping us, we can jump into the car and come back."

Nancy packed her clothing that night. As she was closing down the lid of the suitcase, her eye fell upon the coded message which lay on the dressing table.

"I probably won't have time to work on it, but it won't hurt to take it along," she decided.

She was abroad early the next morning for she intended to go to the next city, pick up Millie and return to River Heights for Bess and George. This would give the girls more time to get ready and would not be out of her way in going to Round Valley, since it was necessary to retrace her ground, anyway.

It was nine-thirty when Nancy reached the city. She stopped at a downtown filling station for gasoline and a change of oil. While the attendant was working over the car, she walked aimlessly about the place, watching the passersby.

"Not a person I know," she said.

Unexpectedly she saw a familiar face.

For an instant, Nancy could not be sure that her eyes were not deceiving her. Yet there was no mistaking that swaggering walk. It was the same girl she had seen a number of days before in the Oriental shop!

The young woman did not glance toward Nancy, but passed the filling station and continued on down the street.

"Now, what can she be doing here?" Nancy asked herself in perplexity.

Motivated by curiosity, she moved over to the sidewalk and stood watching the girl. She saw her enter an office building a short distance farther down the street.

"Now, that looks queer," Nancy thought. "I believe that is the very place where Millie applied for a position!"

A quick glance assured her that the filling station attendant was still working on her car. She would have time to do a bit of investigating!

Hurrying down the street, Nancy entered the building. The corridors were deserted. Evidently the girl had gone into one of the offices, but which one was a mystery. As Nancy stood uncertainly staring up and down, she caught sight of the janitor.

"Did you see a girl come into the building just a moment ago?" she inquired.

"Squint-eyed?" the man demanded, resting on his broom.

Nancy nodded eagerly.

"Yes, she's part Chinese. French-Chinese, I'd judge."

"Oh, you mean Yvonne Wong!"

"You know her, then?"

"No, but I heard that agent she works for, with the loud voice and the swell clothes, call her by that name."

"Oh, she works here, does she?" Nancy inquired in surprise.

"She's one of the new girls. Came here a couple of days ago."

"I see," Nancy murmured, thinking that Yvonne Wong had accomplished a rather sudden change of occupation. "In which office does she work?"

Her questions had commenced to annoy the janitor. He frowned discouragingly as he responded gruffly:

"In 305. If you're so interested, why don't you step in and ask her what you want to know?"

"Thank you," Nancy responded with a polite smile, turning away. "I'll not trouble you any more."

Before she had taken a dozen steps she thought of another question which she felt she must ask.

"Oh, by the way," she said in a tone she tried to make sound casual, "what sort of concern is in that office?"

The janitor regarded her suspiciously.

"How should I know?" he demanded bluntly. "They don't pay me to go stickin' my nose in other folks' business. I got work of my own to do."

Nancy saw that she would learn nothing more, so left the building. She now felt certain that she could not be mistaken. Yvonne Wong was the same girl who only a few days before had been employed in the Oriental perfume shop. Why had she changed positions?

"I wonder how she happened to hear of the opening here?" Nancy mused as she thoughtfully made her way back to the gasoline station. "It looks rather odd, to say the least!"

Again she considered the strange telephone call which had been made while she and Millie were in the office. She distinctly remembered that some mention had been made of a girl who had been found for the position, and that the man who called himself "Al" had remarked that one "couldn't be too careful." Undoubtedly, Yvonne had not secured the position by chance. She had been sought as one especially suitable for the situation.

"There's something underhanded about the affair, but what it is, I haven't the faintest idea," Nancy told herself. "If I weren't going to Red Gate Farm, I might do a little investigating."

It was growing late, and she dared tarry no longer, if the trip to Round Valley were to be made that day. Paying the attendant, she backed her car out into the street and drove rapidly toward Millie's boarding house.

Millie was waiting for her when she arrived. Nancy quickly explained her plan and was not only relieved that the girl offered no objection, but that she seemed pleased with the new scheme.

"It will be jolly fun, all going together," she declared enthusiastically, "and Grandmother will be delighted to have you stay as long as you will."

"Only on the condition that we are paying guests," Nancy insisted.

"We'll see about that later," Millie smiled. "Grandmother says there's enough to worry about, without crossing bridges."

They tossed her suitcase into the back seat of the sedan and soon were speeding back to River Heights. Nancy's stop at the office building had delayed her, and she found Bess and George already waiting. Assured by Millie that they would be more than welcome at Red Gate Farm, they brought out their suitcases and added them to the mounting pile of luggage. They listened to last minute advice from fond parents and then were off.

"What made you take so long to get here,

Nancy?" Bess asked after they had settled themselves for the long ride. "I was beginning to think you'd had an accident."

"I had to stop for gasoline and oil," Nancy returned. She hesitated and then added, "It took me longer than I anticipated due to an unexpected discovery."

"You're always making discoveries!" George remarked. "What is it this time? Did you find a gold mine in the heart of the city?"

"Well, I learned that another girl has the job Millie wanted."

"We guessed that before," George said. "Was that all you discovered?"

"No," Nancy smiled, "I learned her name, too. Isn't that interesting?"

"It really doesn't make much difference now," Millie said with a tired sigh. "I don't hold her any grudge. She probably is better qualified for the position than I am."

"I'm not so sure about that," Nancy returned dryly. "At least, you're not qualified in the same way."

"You were going to tell us the girl's name," George reminded. "Do we know her?"

"I think you do. Her name is unusual—it's Yvonne Wong."

"I don't know any Chinese girls," George protested. "Who is she?"

Nancy did not take her eyes from the road as she returned evenly:

"I'm almost positive she is the same girl who waited upon us at that Oriental perfume shop."

"Really!" Bess exclaimed. "I don't see why they should hire a girl like that! And she already had a position, too."

"She was an insolent thing," George added. "Millie outshone her a million miles! Why, the way she looked down on us, one might think she was heiress to a throne."

"It's nice of you to say it," Millie smiled, "but I'm afraid I didn't measure up."

"It wasn't your fault you didn't get the position," Nancy insisted. "Why, this girl Yvonne Wong isn't in your class at all. She's cheap and loud. There's simply no accounting for tastes, that's all."

Since the matter of employment was an embarrassing one to Millie, the girls tactfully dropped the subject, and chatted on less personal topics. Gradually she responded to their attempts to cheer her, and before they had traveled many miles seemed to have forgotten her unpleasant experiences in the city.

She took a keen interest in the countryside and astonished the girls with her knowledge of nature lore. Millie seemed a different person now that she was away from the depressing effects of the city.

"I guess I was homesick," she confessed as they drove along. "I know I should never have been happy in the city. If only Granny and I can make ends meet!"

"Don't worry," Bess told her. "You'll have three steady boarders for a few weeks at least, and by the time we leave perhaps something will turn up."

After the first few minutes Nancy said very little, paying strict attention to the driving, as there were many cars on the road, and she felt the responsibility of her position as chauffeur.

The others, noticing her serious expression, assumed that she was absorbed in her driving. Could they have followed her thoughts, which centered about such puzzling and diversified matters as secret codes, help for Millie Burd, Oriental perfume, and mysterious office girls, they would have been surprised, indeed!

CHAPTER VII

A Roadside Stop

NANCY and her friends thoroughly enjoyed the long ride to Round Valley. The winding road led through cool groves and skirted enchanting little lakes. Each hilltop brought a new and more delightful scene.

As the heavy sedan sped farther and farther from the city, Millie breathed deeply of the fresh air and relaxed. Gradually, the worried expression left her thin face and she began to laugh heartily at the sallies made by Bess and George.

"How good it will seem to get back to Red Gate Farm again," she murmured.

As they rode, Millie told the girls a great deal about her home.

"You'll like Red Gate, I'm sure," she declared enthusiastically. "We haven't any ponies to ride but there will be plenty of other things to do. We can explore the cave, for one thing."

"Cave?" the girls questioned with interest. "How exciting. What kind is it, a home for

59

bears? Or is it full of bats, or perhaps it's a pirate's den?"

Millie laughed.

"There's a large cavern located on the farm. No one knows how it came to be there but we think it must have been made a long time ago by an underground river."

"Surely you have explored it before this!" Nancy exclaimed.

"Oh, yes, of course, though I'll admit that I never did it very thoroughly, and I haven't been near the cave for years. As a child I was always afraid of the place—it looked so dark and gloomy. Lately, I've been too busy doing other things."

"We must explore the place by all means," George declared. "I like spooky things."

"Well, I don't," Bess announced.

"Maybe we can find a hidden treasure in the walls," Nancy laughed.

"I wish you could," Millie smiled.

The sun had climbed high in the heavens, and before long the girls realized that it was past luncheon time.

"I'm half starved," George announced.

"We might stop at the next town," Nancy suggested. "Take a look at the map, Bess, and see how soon we come to one."

Bess studied the map for a minute or two and then said:

"Galton comes next, I think, and my guess is that it's nearly fifteen miles away! Oh, that's a long way."

"We'll starve before we get there," George grumbled.

"Let's watch for a roadside stand," Nancy proposed. "I'll have to stop soon anyway for more gas."

The girls watched the road and soon sighted a combination filling station and lunch place which looked clean and inviting. Nancy turned the car into the driveway and parked it out of the way of other travelers who might wish to stop for gasoline.

"You must be dead tired," Millie said sympathetically to Nancy. "It would kill me to drive so long without stopping to rest."

"I don't mind it," Nancy laughed. "I am a little tired, but after I've had a square meal, I'll feel like driving forever!"

The girls entered the lunch room and took seats at one of the small white tables. The menu was not especially attractive, so they all decided upon sandwiches, hot cocoa and ice cream sundaes decorated with double portions of chocolate and nuts.

"That means another pound added to my weight," Bess sighed as she gave her order, "but I'd as soon be dead as to give up sundaes!"

Though the girls were the only ones in the lunch room, the woman in charge was extremely slow in filling the orders. Twice Nancy glanced at her watch. At last she arose and went toward the door.

"If you'll excuse me," she said, "I'll step outside and tell the man to fill my gasoline tank. It will save us a little delay in getting started."

"Hurry, then," Bess advised. "I think our order is almost ready."

"Don't wait for me," Nancy advised.

She drove the sedan over to the gasoline pump and told the attendant to fill the tank. Before he could comply with the order, however, a large, high-powered touring car swept up to the other pump, coming to a sudden halt.

"Give me five and make it snappy!" a voice called out impatiently.

The attendant glanced inquiringly at Nancy Drew.

"Do you mind?" he asked.

"Wait on them first if you like," she said politely.

She surveyed the travelers with interest. There were three men in the car, rather rough in appearance, although they wore good clothes. Nancy could not see the face of the driver for it was turned away from her.

Undoubtedly she would have paid no more

attention, had not something happened which served to impress the travelers upon her in a more forceful way.

"I'm going inside and get a couple bottles of ginger ale," she heard the driver grumble to his companions.

As he stepped from the automobile, Nancy saw his face for the first time. It was the stranger who had accosted her on the train! What was even more significant—she detected a faint odor of the familiar perfume.

For some reason which she could not have explained even to herself, Nancy did not wish to be recognized. She turned her head quickly and pretended to be studying a road map.

When the driver had vanished inside the lunch room, she surveyed the two men who remained in the automobile. They were the sort which Carson Drew would have described by the term "tough customers."

She had scant opportunity to study them, for the driver of the car came out of the lunch room with the cold drinks. He did not glance in Nancy's direction, but addressed the attendant in a harsh voice.

"Say, ain't you finished yet? We don't want to stick around here all day!"

He turned to one of the men in the automobile and handed him the two bottles of ginger ale.

"Hold these, will you, Hank? I got to pay this bird!"

Nancy started. Hank! She had heard the name before. She pondered for a moment, and then the answer flashed into her mind.

"That man in room 305 called one of his friends 'Hank' over the telephone," she told herself. "By any chance could they be the same person?"

Her attention was drawn back to the driver who was paying his gasoline bill.

"How much do I owe you?" he demanded of the attendant.

"A dollar ten."

The driver took a thick roll of bills from his pocket, and with a careless gesture peeled off a twenty.

"Aren't you afraid to carry such a wad as that around, sir?" the attendant questioned, gazing admiringly at the thick roll.

The driver laughed boisterously.

"Plenty more where it comes from, eh, Hank?"

"You bet!" was the prompt answer. "My roll makes his look like a flat tire! Just feast your eyes on this!"

He brought out a wad of bills which in truth was larger than that of his companion, flashing it before the amazed eyes of the envious attendant.

"I wish I had that much money," the filling station man said with a sigh. "I'll have to go inside to get your change."

The moment he had disappeared the third man in the car muttered to his companions:

"You fools! Do you want to make him suspicious? Pipe down!" He spoke so low that Nancy would have missed it, had not the wind been in her direction.

"Maurice is right," the driver admitted. "The fellow is only a country yokel but we can't be too careful."

The attendant returned with the change. The driver pocketed it and without another word started the car and drove away.

CHAPTER VIII

Red Gate Farm

"Some class, eh?" the filling station man remarked to Nancy as he came back to her sedan. "Those fellows must be millionaires to have all that money."

Nancy made no response. As soon as her own gasoline tank had been filled, she paid the bill and hurried back into the lunch room. The girls had already been served.

"We took your advice and didn't wait," Bess apologized. "What made it take you so long?"

"Another car drove up and I had to wait a few minutes."

"Our cocoa was getting cold," George explained. "I hope you'll excuse us for our bad manners."

"Oh, I'm glad you didn't wait," Nancy returned, her mind on another matter.

She sat down, thoughtfully nibbling at a sandwich.

"What's the matter with you?" George demanded presently. "You've hardly said a

word since we left River Heights. We're on
a vacation now, so you mustn't be so serious."

Nancy aroused herself and after that entered into the general conversation. As soon
as she had finished her luncheon, they arose to
depart. Nancy insisted upon paying.

"I want to break this twenty-dollar bill Dad
gave me," she offered as her excuse. "I intended to do it before we left home but I forgot
all about it."

The cashier changed the bill for her without
comment and the girls left the lunch room. As
they climbed into the sedan, Nancy glanced
anxiously at the sky.

"It's just as well we're starting," she remarked. "I don't like the appearance of those
clouds overhead."

"It does look like rain," Bess observed anxiously. "Is the road paved all the way to Red
Gate Farm, Millie?"

"No, we leave the main road about six miles
before we get there."

"How much farther is it?" George asked.

"It will take us at least three hours from
here if we don't run into rain," Millie informed her.

"I think we'll run into it," Nancy said as
she started the car.

The sun continued to shine as brightly as
before, and after a time the girls forgot their

fears. Soon they noticed a change in the character of the countryside. The hills became steeper, the valleys deeper. Even if the land in this section of the state were less valuable, the farms were more attractive from a scenic standpoint.

"Perhaps your grandmother will have enough guests without us," Nancy remarked as they drove along.

"Indeed not," Millie assured her promptly. "We have plenty of room at the farm and I'll be there to help with the work."

The girls made fast time, for Nancy was bent upon pushing through before the storm broke. However, after they had been driving for about an hour, she observed that the sky was becoming more overcast.

"We're running straight into it," she told her companions. "Let's hope it will be only a shower."

Soon the afternoon sun was blotted from sight and then the first raindrops appeared on the windshield. The girls quickly closed up the car windows.

"We're in for a regular downpour," Nancy declared grimly.

In a few minutes the highway was wet and slippery and she was forced to drive slowly to avoid skidding. Soon the thunder and lightning began, and the rain came down in torrents.

"I don't like storms like this," Bess complained. "Goodness, listen to that wind. It's enough to blow the car off the road!"

When Nancy came to a stretch of highway which ran through a woodland of tall trees, she was forced to stop. The daylight had been entirely blotted out, and even with the headlights of the car turned on, the road could not be seen.

"Let's turn on the lights inside of the car, then we won't have to look at the lightning."

As George said this a jagged streak of fire came down out of the sky and hit a big oak a short distance from the car, splintering the tree.

"Oh," screamed Bess, "this is terrible. What shall we do?"

"Funny we didn't feel the shock," commented George.

"You can thank the rubber tires on the sedan for that," announced Nancy.

While she was trying to appear calm, she did not feel secure by any means, and decided that it would be safer not to remain near trees which might crash down upon them.

"How long is this stretch of woods?" she asked Millie.

"Oh, not long. Perhaps five hundred feet."

Nancy at once started the motor, and drove as quickly as she dared in the darkness.

All the girls breathed a sigh of relief, when

open country was reached, but in a minute a new fear assailed them.

"Watch out," advised Millie. "We turn very soon. I'm afraid the narrow road will be muddy and slippery."

The thunder and lightning had now moved off to a distant sky, so Nancy was able to discern the corner, where a dilapidated sign indicated the direction to Round Valley. Moreover, she spied a shed and drove into this.

"What now?" demanded George.

"I think we better put chains on," Nancy answered. "Who wants to help?"

Millie insisted that she should be the one, though Bess and George would have gladly helped. The work of putting the chains on did not improve the appearance of the dresses of the young workers, and their hands were stained from the mud.

As Nancy turned in the direction of Round Valley, she found that Millie had been right, and even with chains on the car, Nancy found it difficult to keep from sliding into the deep ditches at the sides of the road. To add to her worry a new storm seemed to be coming up. In less than five minutes darkness descended again, bringing with it a deluge of rain and deafening thunder which followed vivid forks of lightning.

The automobile crept along at a snail's pace,

but it was impossible to see more than twenty-five feet ahead. As the sedan moved up to the brow of a hill, there was a very brilliant flash of lightning. George, who was sitting in the front seat, screamed.

"Oh, don't hit her!"

Nancy jambed on the brakes so quickly that the rear of the car skidded around sideways in the road.

"Who?" the girls demanded.

"The woman in the road. Didn't you see her? Oh, maybe she's under the car!"

Nancy jumped from the automobile by one door, Bess from another. They peered under the car, alongside of it, in back of it. They could see no one.

"Are you sure you saw a woman?" Nancy inquired.

Just then another bit of lightning illumined the scene, and Bess called out:

"There goes a woman across that field."

The four girls sighed with relief. Nancy felt shaken, but managed to ask, as she started the car again:

"Where would anyone be going in such a storm?"

"She's headed in the direction of the cavern," said Millie. "Maybe she's one of those queer people over there!"

CHAPTER IX

A NEWSPAPER ACCOUNT

NANCY DREW and her friends did not have time to question Millie about the queer people. The storm had suddenly passed over, and as the car reached the crest of a steep hill, Millie pointed toward the valley in front of them.

"You can see Red Gate Farm from here!"

The girls looked down upon the forty acres which comprised the farm and thought that it was by far the most attractive one they had seen on their journey. They were less concerned with the fertility of the soil than they were with the picturesque rocks, the groves of pine trees, the winding river which curled along the valley. Everything looked green and fresh after the shower.

"Isn't it beautiful?" Bess asked.

As the automobile descended into the valley, the girls caught a better glimpse of the huge red barn, the various outbuildings and the large rambling farmhouse which was covered with vines. Bright red geraniums peeped from the window ledges; a freshly-painted picket fence

72

surrounded the yard, giving a home-like and hospitable look.

Nancy halted the sedan in front of the big red gate which opened into the garden. Millie sprang out to unbar it, and Nancy drove in.

The door opened and a gray-haired old lady, neat as a pin in her bright gingham dress and white apron, came hurrying out to meet them. Her little blue eyes were very bright as she clasped Millie tightly in her arms.

"My granddaughter wrote me how kind you all were to her in the city," she said to Nancy and her friends. "I can't thank you enough. Millie is so inexperienced and needs looking after, I'm sure."

The girls were somewhat embarrassed by the profuse praise which Mrs. Samantha Burd showered upon them. It was plain to be seen that she loved Millie as her own child, and that Millie's friends were hers. Even before anything was said about Nancy and her chums staying at Red Gate, she invited them to remain.

"Oh, I really don't like to accept any money," she protested. "You have been so kind to my poor Millie——"

"If you won't accept us as paying guests, then we'll have to return home tomorrow," Nancy insisted.

In the end Mrs. Burd gave in. She appeared

very happy as she bustled about helping Millie prepare the rooms. Soon the odor of hot biscuits, sizzling ham, sweet potatoes and coffee came from the kitchen, making the girls realize how hungry they were. Nancy and her friends were not content to be guests but insisted upon helping Millie and her grandmother with the work.

Supper was a delightful affair, for Mrs. Burd knew how to make the girls feel at home. They were ashamed of their appetites, but Mrs. Burd declared that she hoped they would have even better ones before they left Red Gate Farm.

"I don't know what has come over the young people lately," she said, half reproachfully. "All the girls are bent upon staying as thin as a rail. Take Millie now—I can't make her eat enough. Perhaps she will do better with you girls here as good examples."

After supper the girls confessed that they were tired, and in a few minutes they excused themselves and retired to their rooms. George and Bess paired together, while Nancy shared Millie's bedroom.

"Oh, how sweet it smells in here," commented Millie.

"Gracious, that is some of that Oriental perfume that was spilled on my clothes in the train," said Nancy. "It certainly is strong."

"Maybe you'll get your three dollars' worth, after all!" laughed Millie.

When Nancy awoke the next morning warm sunlight was streaming in at the window, and sparrows were chirping excitedly. She sat up in bed, and realized that Millie had already gone.

With a feeling of guilt, she bounded from bed and hurriedly dressed. Knowing that Bess and George would not arise until called, she pounded loudly on the wall which separated their rooms, and was rewarded by hearing George groan.

"Do you mean to sleep away all of your vacation?" Nancy called.

It was only eight o'clock when the three girls went downstairs, but the sun was so bright they were convinced that their watches must be wrong.

Millie and her grandmother sat down at the breakfast table with their guests. The meal was simple but delicious. The girls did ample justice to the fresh berries which floated in thick, rich cream, and Bess did not attempt to disguise the fact that she ate seven large pancakes.

"More weight!" her friends commented.

Millie took the girls on a tour of exploration. She showed them her flowers, her chickens, and

even her pet goat. A turkey gobbler took of-
fense at Bess, and to the delight of the others
forced her to seek refuge on the porch of the
farmhouse.

"Silly! There's nothing to be afraid of,"
Millie laughed as she chased the gobbler away.
"He wouldn't hurt a baby."

Bess looked crestfallen.

"Our farm isn't very well stocked," Millie
admitted, as she led the way to the barn. "We
keep only six cows, and one old work horse.
Poor old Maud should be retired on a pension
but Granny can't afford it yet."

Millie joyfully hailed the hired man.

Reuben Snodgrass, red of hair and decidedly
reticent in manner, acknowledged each introduction with a mumbled "Please to meet you,
Miss," extending a gnarled hand which he permitted each girl to shake in turn. He could
think of nothing to say and stood shifting un-
comfortably from one foot to the other. Millie
took pity on him and permitted him to retreat
to the barn.

"Reuben is as good as gold, even if he is
bashful," Millie told the girls. "I don't know
what Granny and I would do without him. He
does the work of two men and we can't afford
to pay him good wages, either."

"We must keep an eye on Bess while we're

here," George declared teasingly. "If we
don't, she'll be breaking another heart."

Bess made a good-natured retort as the girls
started for the orchard. Here George demon-
strated her prowess by climbing an apple tree.

Millie finally ended her personally-conducted
tour at the big Red Gate where the girls perched
themselves on the top.

"What were you telling us about a cave?"
Nancy questioned curiously. "Didn't you say
there's one on the farm?"

"Yes," Millie returned, "but it's on the piece
of land Granny rents out."

"Oh, I didn't know your grandmother rented
part of her farm," Nancy murmured. "I suppose it will be impossible for us to visit the
cavern then."

"Well, it's on the rented property, but I
don't see why we shouldn't go there if we wish
to," Millie frowned thoughtfully. "It's
Granny's land! Still, they are a queer lot of
people who are there."

"They?" Nancy questioned.

"Yes, the land is leased by some sort of sect.
It's a Nature cult, I believe. As I understand
it, this is merely one colony of a large organization—so it said in the letter Granny received
from their leader. Anyway, this group calls
itself the Black Snake Colony."

"Pleasant name," Bess observed with distaste. "Ugh! I hate snakes! Horrid crawly old things, slipping around."

"I think that's just a name," Millie continued. "I have no idea why they selected it, nd Granny was so glad to have a little income, she made no inquiries."

"You say the people belong to a Nature cult?" Nancy asked curiously. "What do they do most of the time?"

"I've never been able to find out," Millie admitted. "I suppose they believe in living an outdoor life, or something like that."

"One can live that way without joining a silly organization," George observed. "I suppose they dance when the dew is on the grass and all that nonsense!"

"I can't say as to the *dew*," Millie smiled, "but they *do* dance!" After this joke had been duly appreciated, she went on more seriously. "It's mostly at night that they're abroad. They dress in queer white robes and flit around waving their arms. I think it's silly. They wear masks, too!"

"Masks?" Nancy asked with interest. "What's the idea of that?"

"Don't ask me. There doesn't seem to be any sense or reason to any of the ritual, as far as I can see."

"Probably isn't any," commented Bess.

"How much land do they rent?" Nancy next questioned.

"Only five acres, but they insisted upon having a piece along the river. They specified that they wanted it to include the cave. We thought that seemed queer, but we felt it best not to ask questions."

"They live in it?" George inquired.

"I don't know. I've often wondered. I'm afraid to go near the cavern alone, but if you girls were along——"

"When can we go?" Nancy demanded with immediate zest for the adventure.

"Well, not until I've spoken to Granny about it," Millie laughed. "We mustn't do anything that would make her lose her tenants. After all, they pay regularly, and we couldn't hope to get as much from any other people."

"How long have you had this cult on your place?" Nancy next inquired.

"About two months. I've never seen any of the members at close range. They go out only at night time."

"Where do they live?" George demanded. "In the cave?"

"No, in shacks and tents near the river. I really know nothing about them."

"It's queer you've never seen any of the members," Nancy remarked thoughtfully. "Who pays the rent?"

"It's sent by mail."

"That *is* queer. Didn't you see any of the members when they first came to rent the place from your grandmother?"

Millie shook her head.

"All the negotiations were carried on by mail."

"Didn't it strike you as rather peculiar they would do business that way?" Nancy asked.

"Yes," Millie admitted, "but I suppose it's part of their creed, or whatever you call it. Probably they don't believe in mingling with persons who are not members of the cult. I've heard that's often the case."

"You never see anyone around?" Bess questioned Millie.

"Only at a distance. There are quite a number of members, though, and I've seen several women. They have their ceremonies at night."

"I hope they have one while we are here," George said.

The girls had a great many more questions which they wished to ask, but just at that moment Mrs. Burd called Millie to help her with the churning.

Left to themselves, Nancy and her chums wandered about the garden, selecting flowers for the dining table.

"You know, if I were Mrs. Burd I wouldn't

want queer folks occupying my farm," George declared flatly.

"Neither would I," Nancy agreed, "but I imagine she is so hard up for cash, she can't afford to be particular."

"I don't believe I want to visit that cave, even if Mrs. Burd thinks it will be all right," Bess said nervously.

Nancy and George laughed at that, for they were both ready for an adventure.

By the time the girls had become fairly well acquainted with their surroundings, the mailman drove up in his car. He hailed Millie by name and dropped two letters into her hand.

"They're both for Granny," Millie said, glancing at the addresses. "I imagine they're from the new boarders she is expecting."

Her guess was correct. The first letter proved to be from a Mrs. Salisbury, saying that her daughter who was employed in the city would bring her to Red Gate Farm the next day. The second letter was from a man by the name of Auerbacher, who planned to arrive sometime later that week.

"Dear me," Mrs. Burd said anxiously. "I didn't expect them so soon. Their rooms aren't ready."

"Don't worry about it," Nancy told her quickly. "We'll all pitch in and help."

Directly after luncheon the girls helped

straighten the rooms and make everything spic and span. Mrs. Burd had made new curtains for the bedrooms and new drapes for the living room, and Nancy and her chums hung them. They filled every vase in the house with flowers. Bess had taken a course in interior decorating, and Mrs. Burd was willing that she should experiment with the furniture to her heart's content. The girls toiled hard all afternoon, but at the end of the day they were satisfied with their work.

"I declare, it does look fine," Mrs. Burd praised them.

While she prepared supper, the girls went out on the veranda to enjoy a well-earned rest. Bess stretched herself in the hammock and picked up a city newspaper which she had not read, though it was several days old. Millie opened a book, while Nancy and George played with Tige, a shepherd dog. They paid no particular attention to Bess until they heard her utter an exclamation of surprise.

"Nancy," she asked tensely, "what was the name of that girl who sold us the perfume?"

"Wong," Nancy answered in surprise. "Yvonne Wong. Why do you ask?"

"Because there's an article in the paper that mentions her name!" Bess thrust the newspaper into Nancy's hands, indicating the paragraph. "Read it for yourself!"

CHAPTER X

THE NEW BOARDERS

"THE paper says that the Hale Syndicate, which has been engaged in illegal importation, has been dissolved by order of Federal authorities," Nancy read. "I certainly cannot see just what that has to do with our perfume friend, Yvonne Wong."

"A great deal," Bess declared. "Read on and you'll find out! Her name is mentioned at the very bottom of the long paragraph about the syndicate."

"My word!" Nancy exclaimed. "Yvonne was employed by the syndicate!"

Bess nodded, feeling very important because of her startling discovery.

"That perfume store that we visited must have been owned by those people."

"How long ago was the syndicate dissolved?" George asked.

"The article doesn't state," Nancy returned, glancing at the date line of the news sheet. "This paper is several days old, too."

"It doesn't surprise me to learn that Yvonne

was mixed up in some underhanded affair,"
Bess remarked. "I didn't like her appearance
from the first!"

"Neither did I," George added, "and I liked
it less after Nancy found out she had received
the position Millie wanted."

"I didn't want it as much as I thought," Millie smiled. "I'd rather be here."

"I wonder if Yvonne knew that she was
working for a dishonest concern," George said
musingly.

"My guess is that she did," Bess insisted.
"However, it looks as though she slipped out
of it quickly, when the federal authorities became aware of what was going on."

"And just what was going on?" Nancy
asked, studying the newspaper thoughtfully.
"The article doesn't say, and that's what I particularly want to know."

"I imagine the government couldn't convict
anyone," George declared. "Otherwise, it
would be stated in the paper. Queer that
Yvonne Wong's name should be mentioned as
an employee."

"She must be under suspicion," Nancy said
thoughtfully.

The discussion ended as Mrs. Burd called the
girls to supper. Before going into the dining
room, Nancy tore the clipping from the paper
and slipped it into her pocket.

Though Nancy did not mention her suspicions to the others, it had instantly occurred to her that Yvonne Wong was still employed by the syndicate, though undoubtedly the name and the offices had been changed to throw the federal authorities off the track. How otherwise could she account for what had transpired in Room 305 on the day she and Millie had called at the office?

"I wish I knew why the syndicate was forced to dissolve," she told herself. "It's very likely they're engaged in the same business now. Yet," she argued, "there wasn't any indication that an importing business was being conducted there—it's beyond me!"

The more she thought of the matter, the more firmly she became convinced that Yvonne Wong had been engaged by employers who knew of her past record. Likewise, she reached the conclusion that the new employers were in some way connected with the old syndicate, but as to the business which was being conducted she could form no definite opinion. For a moment she wished that she was back in River Heights!

Nancy had brought the coded telephone message with her, but the girls had been so busy that she had not had time to study it.

"I must get at it again," she told herself. "The message has more significance now than ever before."

She was too tired to work on it that night, and the next day everyone's attention was occupied with the new boarder.

Shortly before luncheon an expensive motor car drove up to the door to deposit Mrs. Alice Salisbury and her daughter Nona. Mrs. Salisbury walked with a cane, and complained loudly of her rheumatism as the girls helped her into the house.

Nona waited only long enough to see that her mother was comfortably established and then announced that she must hurry back.

"Mother was born on a farm," she told Mrs. Burd as she stepped into her car, "and she simply pines for the country. Since she couldn't be entirely happy with me in the city, I thought this arrangement might prove ideal. I live close enough so that I can drive down to see her on week-ends. I do hope Mother will be happy here at Red Gate Farm."

Millie and her friends hoped so too, but they were not at all certain, for it became increasingly apparent that old Mrs. Salisbury could not be happy anywhere. She had no fault to find with the immaculate farmhouse and even became mildly enthusiastic as she surveyed the splendid view from her bedroom window, but her various aches and pains kept her miserable. She was an inveterate talker and loved to tell

the girls of her many operations. She had a
cryptic tongue and delighted to use it.

"She wouldn't be so bad, if only she'd stop
talking operations," George burst out. "When
she goes into all the harrowing details, it almost makes me feel as though I'm ready for
the hospital myself!"

By the time the girls had adjusted themselves
to Mrs. Salisbury's presence in the house, the
second boarder arrived. It was Karl Auerbacher, a gruff man, who, in spite of his sixty-
eight years, boasted that he was as spry as his
son Karl Jr. He pinched Millie's thin cheek
playfully and praised everything. Karl Jr.,
who was employed in a nearby city, was quite
handsome, and the girls were sorry that he
could not remain with his father.

"I can't leave my business for more than a
day at a time," he told them regretfully.
"Wish I could. This place is attractive."

The girls liked Mr. Auerbacher very much,
but they were appalled at his appetite.

"I wish we could turn him out in the yard to
forage for himself, like the goat," Millie sighed
one day as she peeled her second heaping pan
of potatoes. "He eats as much as all the rest
of us put together."

At first Mr. Auerbacher showed a disposition
to linger about the kitchen, teasing the girls as

they worked and frequently "sampling" various dishes. When Millie and her grandmother
discouraged this, he fell into the habit of sitting
on the front porch with Mrs. Salisbury. To
the intense relief of the girls they became
friendly, and were satisfied to chat together by
the hour. Frequently they would indulge in
violent arguments about inconsequential things.
After one of their disagreements Mrs. Salisbury would maintain a stony silence which was
refreshing, but Mr. Auerbacher would again put
in his appearance in the kitchen.

"You know, I've decided to rename the
goat," Millie told her friends one day when
the old boarder had been particularly annoying.
"I'm going to call him Karl because he's always butting into things!"

In spite of various slight annoyances, the
days at Red Gate Farm passed very pleasantly.
Nancy would dash to town in her car and bring
back the mail—an act very much appreciated
by the boarders. One particular day she had
sped into town, gathered the contents of the
local post office box, and returned without sorting over the pile, in order to be in time for the
lesson in milking Reuben Snodgrass had promised to give.

She jumped out of the car and quickly doled
out letters to everyone's satisfaction. One un-
claimed envelope had slipped unwittingly into

the pile. It bore the Black Snake Colony address.

"Look, girls!" exclaimed Nancy. "It belongs over the hill. The clerk inserted it in our box."

"What will you do?" questioned Bess seriously as she thought of the queer cult in the cave. "Will you drive over with it?"

"Of course not," growled Mr. Auerbacher forcibly. "You keep away from those outrageous people. Take it to the post office tomorrow."

Nancy studied the postmark. It was very blurred. Could it be Riverside Heights, or was she mistaken? She got no further, for just then a neighbor passed. Mrs. Burd handed the letter to him to re-mail, and Nancy was relieved from further responsibility.

She felt a bit disappointed, but went off with the other girls to the stable. She forgot the postmark for the time being, as the "city gals," as Reuben called them, were ready for their lesson in milking.

"Pooh! It's no trick at all," Bess insisted. "Give me that pail and I'll show you just how to do it. Why, it's as easy as can be."

Reuben handed over the bucket, and Bess marched determinedly up to the cow.

"Nice bossy, nice bossy," she murmured, giving the animal a timid pat on the neck.

Bossy responded with a suspicious look and a wicked flirt of her tail. As Bess set the milking-stool down upon the stable floor, the cow aimed a kick at it.

Bess sprang back in alarm.

"You can't expect me to milk a vicious cow!" she exclaimed.

Millie and Reuben exploded with laughter.

"Bossy is about as vicious as that old turkey gobbler you're so scared of," Reuben told her.

"She was trying to kick me! I suppose you call that nothing but friendly interest! I didn't bargain to milk such a beast."

"Bossy's a smart cow," Reuben drawled. "She won't stand being milked from the wrong side."

"Wrong side!" Bess exploded. "Whoever heard of a cow with a right or wrong side?"

"You made the same mistake at Shadow Ranch," George teased, "only it was a horse, then."

"I don't see what difference it makes," Bess protested. "The milk tastes the same."

Reluctantly she picked up the overturned stool and went around to the other side, whereupon the cow leisurely moved herself sideways.

"I tell you this cow doesn't like me! Here, you try it, George."

"It's no trick at all to milk, so you go ahead!"

After a great deal of maneuvering Bess succeeded in seating herself in the correct position, but it was not until Reuben had offered additional instruction that she finally obtained a thin stream of milk from the annoyed cow.

Nancy came last, and profited by the instruction furnished the others, but she, too, was awkward. When Reuban sat down to milk, the girls regarded him with more admiration than previously.

That evening Mrs. Salisbury and Mr. Auerbacher announced they would retire early. Mrs. Burd soon followed, leaving the girls alone on the porch.

"What a heavenly night," Bess sighed contentedly. "Did you ever see such a big moon, girls?"

"It makes everything almost as bright as day," Nancy said. "I like to look way out over the hills. They're so——"

She broke off suddenly and sprang to her feet. The others regarded her with startled wonder.

"Tell me, am I seeing things?" Nancy demanded tensely. "Look, girls, over there on that hilltop!"

Following her gaze, the girls were astonished to see shadowy white figures flitting about in the moonlight.

"Ghosts!" Bess exclaimed.

"Ghosts nothing," George retorted. "Such things don't exist."

"Don't be alarmed, girls," Millie said with a smile. "I imagine the members of the Nature cult are having one of their numerous airings. You never see them out in their white robes except on bright nights."

The girls sat down on the porch steps to watch the cult members go through their mystic rites.

"They're not doing much of anything," Nancy observed. "They just flit around."

Within ten minutes the ceremony was concluded. The girls saw the white figures vanish over the brow of the hill.

"It didn't last very long," Bess complained. "I wonder if the ritual has any significance?"

"That's what I'd like to know," Nancy said quietly as the girls made their way into the house. "I mean to find out, too!"

CHAPTER XI

WARNINGS

EVER since the day of her arrival at Red Gate Farm Nancy had been possessed of an over-whelming desire to visit the cavern on the hill-side. The strange moonlight ceremony which she had witnessed only served to intensify her interest in the place. She felt certain that the cave must be used in some way by the members of the mysterious Nature cult.

The girls had broached the subject to Mrs. Burd of such a visit, and while she had not forbidden the adventure, she had frowned upon it as not advisable.

"I'll worry if you go there," she declared. "Those folks are probably harmless, but we don't know much about them. I wish now I had never rented the land. The neighbors are saying I was foolish to do it."

"And so you were!" Mrs. Salisbury, who was sitting on the front porch as usual and had overheard the conversation, chimed in. "You'll damage the value of your farm."

"We can't sell it, anyway," Millie smiled,

"and it's ridiculous what folks are saying about the people out there. Why, even Reuben is afraid to go near the place!"

"I'm not," Nancy announced. "I think it would be fun to investigate."

Mrs. Salisbury snorted.

"Fun! Girls these days have strange ideas of fun! When I was young they didn't run around like tomboys! First thing you know, Mrs. Burd, they'll be joinin' the cult!"

"I'm not worried about that," Mrs. Burd smiled. "These girls are a sensible lot of young folks, in my opinion."

As a result of the conversation the girls did not visit the cavern; neither did they give up the plan.

"We may talk Granny around to our way of thinking if we can only keep Mrs. Salisbury from interfering," Millie declared. "She's always advising against anything exciting."

The girls decided that they could afford to bide their time for a few days, especially as there were many other things to occupy their time. They had become wildly enthusiastic over farm life, and wrote long letters home to their relatives begging for extensions to their vacations. As they had hoped, their requests were immediately granted.

One afternoon when the others were too indolent to go with her, Nancy set out on a long tramp by herself. Making her way to the woods which skirted the river, she struck a well-worn path and decided to follow it.

She had walked only a short way when from a distance she heard a faint cry as from one in distress. Nancy halted in the path and listened intently. The cry was not repeated.

"Perhaps I imagined it," she told herself, "or it may have been a bird or a wild animal."

Nevertheless, she quickened her pace. Rounding a bend a few minutes later she was startled to see an old woman hunched over on the ground, writhing with pain.

"What is the matter?" Nancy cried, hurrying to her.

"I tripped over a vine in the path," the old woman murmured, rocking back and forth in her agony. "My ankle—it's broken."

Nancy dropped down on one knee and quickly examined the injured ankle. It was rapidly swelling, but all the bones seemed to be in place.

"See if you can stand," she advised.

With Nancy's help the old woman managed to get to her feet, but she winced as she attempted to take the first step.

"It isn't broken," Nancy declared in relief, "but you have a bad sprain."

"I dunno what I'll do now," the old woman moaned.

"Do you live far from here?' Nancy asked.

The woman looked at her rather queerly and did not answer at once. Nancy thought she had not understood, so repeated the question.

"About a quarter of a mile up the river," was the mumbled response. "I'll get there."

"You're scarcely able to walk a step," Nancy said with a troubled frown. "I'll tell you what I'll do. I'll run back to the farm and bring help."

"No, no," the woman cried instantly, clutching Nancy fearfully by the arm. Realizing that the refusal of help might look strange, she added hastily, "I don't want to be a trouble to anyone."

"Nonsense! You shouldn't be walking on that foot at all. It won't take me a minute to run back to the farm."

The old woman shook her head stubbornly.

"My foot feels better now. I can walk by myself."

She started off, but nearly collapsed by the time she had taken three steps.

"If you won't let me go for help, then at least I mean to aid you in getting back to your home."

The woman protested but Nancy took hold of her arm, placing it over her own shoulder. Thus supported, the woman made slow and painful progress up the path. She endured the agony stoically and only once uttered a cry of pain.

"This is killing you," Nancy said, distressed that the woman was so foolishly stubborn. "I can get the hired man to carry you——"

"No!" came the vehement reply.

Nancy could not understand the old woman's unwillingness to accept help. As they made their way slowly up the path, she became aware that her companion's distress was not entirely due to pain, but partially to her own presence. This mystified her, but she could not bring herself to turn back as long as the old woman really needed her. Perhaps, after all, she was an eccentric person.

"I don't remember seeing any houses along the river," Nancy said after a time. "You're not a member of the Nature cult, are you?"

A half-cynical expression passed over the old woman's face, to be replaced almost instantly by one of sadness.

"Yes," she returned quietly, "I'm one of the members."

Nancy surveyed her companion more critically than before. She wore a blue gingham dress which, though plain and durable, did not have the appearance of a costume. The woman did not speak or act as Nancy imagined a member of a cult would. She had thought of these strange folk as somewhat fanatical, but her companion seemed like any other person.

"It must be healthful to live an outdoor life," Nancy remarked, feeling that some comment was necessary. "I've often looked over at your tents and thought I should like to visit the Colony some time."

The old woman stopped abruptly in the path and faced Nancy, a queer look on her wrinkled countenance.

"You must never come near!"

"Why not?"

"It wouldn't be safe!"

"Not safe!" Nancy echoed in astonishment. "I don't understand."

"I—I mean the members of the cult don't want folks prying around," the woman said hastily.

"I see. The rites are secret."

"That's it," the other returned in relief.

"But why couldn't I visit the colony sometime when ceremonies aren't being held?" Nancy persisted.

"You mustn't come near—ever!"

The two continued up the path. To Nancy it was apparent that her questions had greatly disturbed the woman, for several times she caught her looking distressed and worried.

As they approached the hillside colony, yet

before they were within sight of the tents, the old woman halted.

"Thank you for your help," she said quietly. "I can make it alone from here."

Nancy hesitated. She felt that the woman was not able to walk by herself, but the firm tone told her that it would do no good to protest. The woman had made up her mind that strangers were not to come near the camp, and that apparently settled the matter.

"At least let me find you a stout stick," Nancy said.

She searched along the path and soon found one which was suitable. The woman accepted it gratefully. Her face softened and she stood for an instant, looking down at Nancy.

"You're a good girl to help an old woman like me. I wish——"

What it was that she wished Nancy never knew, for the woman turned abruptly away.

"Remember," she advised sternly over her shoulder, "don't ever come near the camp!"

Sorely perplexed, Nancy watched the old woman hobble away. It took her a long time to reach the top of the hill and several times she paused to rest. At last she disappeared.

"I can't understand why the poor thing acted the way she did," Nancy told herself as she sat down on a log to think. "It was torture for her to walk; yet she would go on by herself. What harm could it have done if I'd gone with her to the Colony? The cult must have some very important secrets!"

For perhaps fifteen minutes she considered the matter, and the more she thought about it, the more baffled she became.

"The woman didn't look as though being a member of the cult made her very happy," she thought. "If they're so afraid that folks will discover their secrets, they must be doing more than just chasing around at night in white robes! Perhaps that's only to keep people from guessing what really goes on there!"

As Nancy reached this startling conclusion, she jumped to her feet and started back toward Red Gate Farm at a brisk walk.

"There's one thing certain," she told herself with a chuckle, "I'm not going to take that old lady's advice. At the first opportunity I intend to visit the camp. Then Nancy Drew will find out what's what!"

CHAPTER XII

An Adventure

WHEN Nancy reached Red Gate Farm, she found Mrs. Salisbury, Mr. Auerbacher and the girls sitting on the front porch. She had not intended to relate her experience, but her face was so animated that it gave her away. They besieged her with questions until at last, realizing what an excellent story it would make, she told of her meeting with the woman member of the strange Nature cult.

"Told you not to come near, did she?" Mrs. Salisbury cackled. "Well, well, I hope you intend to follow her advice."

Nancy laughed and shook her head.

"I'm more interested than ever in what's going on up there on the hillside. I think it would be jolly fun to investigate."

"So do I," George chimed in.

Millie nodded vigorously, while Bess gave a half-hearted one, for she was naturally timid. Although she loved adventure as well as did her chums, she was always cautious.

"Better stay away," Mr. Auerbacher advised, agreeing for once with Mrs. Salisbury. "You can't tell what may be going on there. My son always says not to meddle with things that don't concern one."

Nancy was tempted to make a sharp retort, for it seemed to her that Mr. Auerbacher and Mrs. Salisbury had nothing else to do than sit on the front porch and offer unnecessary advice. However, she smiled sweetly and said:

"It seems to me that this matter may be of deep concern to Millie and her grandmother, if not to me."

Mrs. Burd had stepped to the porch door in time to gather the gist of the conversation, and at once spoke up.

"I don't know but that Nancy is right," she declared thoughtfully. "Of course, I don't want the girls to go looking for trouble, but I'm beginning to think someone ought to investigate the doings up there on the hill. If anything is going on that isn't right, I want to know about it. I'll turn the folks away even if I do lose the rent. Why, I might get into trouble, myself."

Mr. Auerbacher and Mrs. Salisbury lapsed into an injured silence. Nancy gave her chums a sly wink, and in a few minutes they all quietly withdrew to the spring house where they held council.

"Strange things are going on at those cult

meetings," Nancy announced, "and I mean to find out about them if I can. Do you girls want to be in on the fun?"

"Of course," Millie and George said.

"Do you think it will be safe to interfere?" Bess asked.

"I'm not making any rash promises," Nancy laughed, "but if I didn't think it was safe I wouldn't jump into the thing. It may be only a silly superstition that those folks have about not letting people come near the place!"

"And it may be something more serious," Bess added with a little shiver. "Nevertheless, count me in on whatever you do."

"It's clear that we'll never get anywhere, if we listen to those two helpful boarders," Nancy went on. "On the other hand we want to go at this thing cautiously."

"How can we visit the Colony without being caught?" George demanded.

"That's the problem. We must lay our plans carefully. Before we do anything, I want to find out about the robes the cult members wear. We may have use for the information later on."

"There is only one way to find that out," Millie said, "and that's to watch some night when they are having a ceremonial meeting. We can sneak through the woods and perhaps get close enough to see what's going on."

Nancy nodded soberly.

"That's what I thought. However, I don't hope to discover much, for it's my opinion that the secret meetings the cult members hold on the hillside are merely to throw people off the track. Perhaps we can find out about the costumes, though."

"I don't know whether I told you or not," Millie broke in, "but that cave has two entrances—one on our property and the other on the hillside which is occupied by the cult."

"You may have mentioned it," Nancy said, "but I had forgotten. The double entrance will be fine! If we can't break into the meetings any other way, we can sneak into the cavern and come out the other side."

"If we have the nerve," Bess added. "It sounds terribly scarey to me!"

"There's nothing definite about the plan yet," Nancy declared. "For a few days we better bide our time. Everyone keep her eyes open and don't let Mrs. Salisbury or Mr. Auerbacher know what we are about or they may talk Mrs. Burd out of the notion of letting us investigate."

The girls maintained a silence concerning the activity of the Nature cult, but their secretive manner aroused the suspicions of the two boarders.

"You're up to something," Mrs. Salisbury

remarked one day, "and if I were Mrs. Burd, I'd put a stop to it at once."

Mrs. Burd, however, went serenely on her way, undisturbed by what the girls were planning, or interfering with their fun.

The days passed swiftly and were very pleasant ones, too, but as far as Nancy and her chums were concerned, they were uneventful. Karl Jr. came to visit his father, and Nona Salisbury spent the week-end with her mother, both returning to the city. Reuben Snodgrass continued to induct the "city gals," as he termed them, into the intricate mysteries of farm life.

Only the Nature cult remained disappointingly inactive. Though the girls maintained a close watch of the hillside, they seldom saw anyone in the vicinity. On starlit nights they were particularly vigilant, hoping to see the members "on dress parade."

"I think they've holed in for the rest of the summer," George declared in disgust one day. "Either that, or they know we're watching for them."

"They're still there," Millie returned, "for the rent check arrived through the mail this morning."

"I saw smoke curling up from one of the tents early today," Bess added.

"By the way," Nancy broke in, addressing

Millie, "where do these folks get their food? They can't live on blue sky and inspiration."

"I think friends must bring food to them in automobiles," Millie answered. "Several times I've seen fine cars drive up and park near the hillside."

"The cult members must be well to do, then," Nancy remarked thoughtfully. "Oh, dear, I'm getting tired of marking time. I wish something would happen soon. If it doesn't, I think I'll venture into that cave!"

Perhaps in answer to her wish, "things" happened that very night.

The girls were late in finishing the dishes, and by the time they had put everything away it was quite dark. Going out to the porch for a breath of cool air, they were relieved to find that the boarders had retired to their rooms. For some minutes they sat chatting. The moon was high and Nancy, from force of habit, glanced eagerly toward the distant hillside.

"Look, girls!" she cried. "They're at it again!"

They could see white objects moving to and fro, apparently going through a weird ritual. Nancy sprang to her feet.

"We'll have to hurry if we mean to see anything," she said. "Come on!"

The four girls rushed across the lawn, hurled themselves over the gate and took to the woods.

Nancy led the way up the river path. Not until they all were close to the camp did she stop.

"We must be very careful," she warned in a whisper. "Scatter and hide behind trees, and keep very quiet."

The girls obeyed, Bess keeping close beside George, for she was afraid. Nancy found a huge oak tree well up the hill, and hid herself behind it. From this advantageous position she was able to see fairly well.

She had been there less than five minutes when she was startled to hear the sound of several approaching automobiles. They came up from the narrow road and stopped at the base of the hill not far from the Nature camp.

Several men stepped from the cars. Nancy was too far away to see their faces, but she did observe that they quickly donned long white robes with head masks, and joined the other costumed figures who were on the brow of the hill.

For nearly ten minutes the members of the cult flitted back and forth, waving their arms and making weird noises. Then they moved single file toward the cavern and vanished within its yawning mouth.

Suddenly Nancy felt herself grasped by an arm. She wheeled sharply about and then laughed softly.

"George! For pity's sake don't ever do that

again! You scared me out of a year's growth!''

"What do you make of it, Nancy?''

"It's the strangest thing I ever saw. I haven't been able to figure it out. I'm wondering what to do next.''

"Tell you what! Let's follow them into the cave,'' George proposed rashly.

"And be caught?'' Nancy returned. "No, this is serious business and we must use judgment. I've seen enough for one night. I think it's time to go home.''

"All right,'' George grumbled.

Bess and Millie were more than willing to turn back, for what they had witnessed had left them somewhat shaky.

"I wonder why so many folks came here in automobiles?'' Millie mused as the girls walked slowly home.

"That's what I wonder, too,'' Nancy replied soberly, "but I think I know.''

"Why?'' her friends demanded.

"Well, of course, this is only a theory, but it looks to me as though only a very few persons are actually living in the Black Snake Colony. They want to give out the impression that the organization is a large one, so they have these other people come the night set for the ceremonials.''

"There were certainly a lot of men in those automobiles,'' added Bess.

"Why should they go to all that bother?" Millie asked doubtfully.

"I don't know," Nancy admitted, "unless it's because they're trying to hide something they are doing here."

"How shall we ever find out unless we explore the cave?" George grumbled. She still wished to go on with the adventure.

"Don't worry, I intend to visit that cave, but I don't mean to rush into danger blindly. I found out what I came for tonight."

"You mean about the costume?" Millie questioned.

Nancy nodded.

"Yes, I think I'll be able to make one if you'll lend me a pillow case and some sheets. When I visit the cavern, I aim to have at least a fighting chance!"

CHAPTER XIII

ANOTHER WARNING

THE next few days at Red Gate Farm were quiet ones. Following the ceremonial meeting held by the members of the Nature cult, the hillside camp appeared very nearly deserted. Occasionally the girls beheld smoke curling up from the vicinity of the tents and shacks, but besides that there was no sign of any life out there.

"Those people must hibernate between ceremonials," George remarked one day. "It certainly beats all how much time they spend in that cave!"

"What puzzles me is what became of those automobiles that were on the hillside the night we watched," Bess said. "I wish we had seen them leave."

Nancy did not discuss the matter as frequently as did her chums, but she spent a great deal of time considering the situation. In fact, so absorbed had she become in the doings of the Nature cult that Yvonne Wong and the queer business which apparently was being conducted in Room 305 tended to slip into the background.

"There's nothing much we can do except wait until the cult holds its next ceremonial meeting," she told her friends when they became slightly impatient at the delayed action. "When that time comes—well, I'll have a plan!"

When pressed for details Nancy would only shake her head. In truth, she did not herself know what she would do when the time came to act. Of only one thing was she certain. She was determined to attend the next ceremonial meeting and follow the members of the cult into the cave.

Mr. Auerbacher and Mrs. Salisbury continued to offer advice and to ask prying questions, but the girls gave them no satisfaction. Millie had spoken to her grandmother concerning the proposed investigation, and she had grudgingly consented that the girls might use their own judgment in the matter.

Nancy and her friends did not spend all their time watching the hillside. They played croquet on the lawn, and although the game was not as exciting as tennis or golf, yet it served to while away the time. Reuben Snodgrass taught them how to play "horseshoe," and then with lack of gallantry defeated them consistently.

The girls enjoyed the outdoor work best of

all. They had a great deal of fun picking the cherries and packing them in boxes which were taken to the nearest town. Each evening they took the shepherd dog and rounded up the cows, frequently helping the hired man with the milking.

One afternoon the girls started for the pasture after the usual hour.

"It is getting late," Millie observed anxiously. "We must hurry!"

They raced across the meadow with the dog barking at their heels. The cows were in the far end of the field.

"Oh, see what's happened!" Millie cried suddenly, halting near the barbed-wire fence. "This post is down. I wonder if any of the cows have strayed?"

As the shepherd dog rounded them up, she counted them anxiously.

"The Jersey is missing," she declared. "Oh, dear, just when we're so late!"

"You girls drive the cows on into the barn," Nancy suggested. "I'll get the Jersey. She couldn't have strayed far."

Millie hesitated, and glancing toward the western horizon she was alarmed to see that the sun was low.

"All right," she agreed. "If you don't find her right away I'll come back and help you hunt."

Nancy slipped through the opening in the fence and dashed off through the woods. She had never been that way before, but there was only one path to follow. Several times she paused to listen and thought she heard the faint tinkling of a cowbell somewhere ahead of her.

It was rapidly growing dark in the woods and Nancy hurried faster. Again she stopped to listen. She could hear the cowbell quite distinctly now.

She hurried on again. Unexpectedly she caught sight of the Jersey contentedly munching the grass on the hillside, entirely unaware that she was upsetting Red Gate Farm.

Nancy stopped short and gave a gasp of astonishment—not because she had found the cow but because she stood facing the yawning mouth of the cave! This was certainly a great piece of luck!

"Well, did you ever!" she exclaimed aloud. "How in the world did I get here? This must be the other opening Millie was telling me about. Undoubtedly the cave runs through to the river, opening near the Nature cult camp!"

Eagerly Nancy rushed forward, bent upon examining the opening. Whether or not she would have had the courage to enter alone she never knew, for no sooner had she peeped into the dark entrance than she was startled by the crackling of a stick behind her. She wheeled and beheld a man standing not three feet away from her!

He seemed to arise from the bushes which half hid the opening of the cave, and instantly it flashed through Nancy's mind that he had been stationed there to see that intruders did not venture inside.

"What you doing here?" a voice, cold as steel, demanded.

Nancy recoiled. The man stood in the shadow so that she could not see his face distinctly, but at the sound of his voice she knew instantly who it was.

It was one of the men she had seen at the filling station—the blustering man who had been addressed as Hank. Nancy was so startled at seeing him again that she could not answer him.

Evidently the man misinterpreted her surprise as fear, for he came toward her menacingly, repeating his question.

"I was hunting for that cow," Nancy returned, pointing to the Jersey which was grazing a short distance away.

She held her ground defiantly, and as the man edged closer she became aware of a familiar odor of perfume. It was the same scent which had attracted her interest in the Oriental shop. She was at the point of asking a pertinent question, but refrained. She told herself that she must be very careful not to arouse the man's suspicions for she was in a dangerous position.

"So you were after the cow?" the lookout growled. "Then why are you by this cave?"

"Why, I was just wondering what was inside," Nancy said innocently. "Surely there's no harm in looking."

"You've no business around here," the man snapped. "This property belongs to the members of the Black Snake Colony."

"Oh!" Nancy exclaimed in pretended awe. "Then you must belong to the Colony. How very interesting."

The man scowled but did not satisfy Nancy's curiosity regarding the matter. Instead, he muttered:

"Round up that old cow of yours and get out of here! Mind you don't come trespassing again, too!"

Nancy knew that she would gain nothing by arguing. She was really a little afraid of the man, for his face was hard and cruel. Obediently she overtook the cow and headed her back toward Red Gate Farm. The man watched until Nancy disappeared into the woods.

However, as soon as she had started the cow down the path Nancy quietly retraced her steps. She reached the edge of the woods just in time to see the man enter the cave.

For an instant Nancy was tempted to follow, but common sense told her that it would be an insane thing to do, for the chances were that she would walk into an ambush.

Reluctantly, she turned back toward Red Gate and her waiting friends. Now Nancy Drew had still more to ponder over. This hillside secret was becoming more mysterious each day!

"I can't understand what that man is doing here," she thought to herself. "He must belong to the Nature cult, and yet I never saw anyone who looked more like a crook!"

It was clear to Nancy that "Hank" had been stationed at the mouth of the cave as a lookout. Obviously the members of the cult were afraid that some of the countryfolk would attempt to investigate. Why were they so careful to maintain secrecy unless they were engaged in an unlawful enterprise? It was all very mysterious and puzzling.

The perfume, too, baffled Nancy. She reviewed the various incidents which had occurred in connection with it.

First, Yvonne Wong had been reluctant to sell her a bottle of it; then on the train a stranger had accosted her, asking if she had received any message from the "Chief." Later she had detected the scent on one of the men who had

driven up to the filling station, and now she
encountered it again.

"What can be the connection?" she asked
herself. "I'm sure there must be one. Is it
possible that all those persons are involved in
some unscrupulous affair?"

Of one thing Nancy was now fairly certain.
The Nature cult was a false organization and
the Colony's activities were used as a cover for
some shady enterprise. It remained for her to
discover what that enterprise was, and who
might be involved.

"In some way Yvonne Wong and that man
she works for are mixed up in it," Nancy told
herself. "If only I could decipher that code I
might be able to solve the mystery!"

It was nearly dark when Nancy reached Red
Gate.

"We were beginning to worry," Millie declared in relief. "I wouldn't have let you go
alone if I'd had any idea that old cow had
strayed so far."

"I'm glad I went," Nancy said quickly.

She then told her friends what had taken
place near the mouth of the cave. However,
she did not mention having seen the man before.

"Those cult people are getting too bossy for
anything!" Millie declared impatiently.

"Weren't you terribly frightened when he sprang up out of the bushes?" Bess asked, giving Nancy an admiring glance. "I'd have fainted on the spot!"

"Girls don't faint these days," George scoffed. "Probably you'd have screamed and that would have brought all the members down upon you. They'd have dragged you off into the cave and put an end to you!"

"Do hush!" Bess pleaded. "You can think of the most blood-curdling things to say! I'll be so nervous I'll be afraid to go near the cave when they hold their next meeting."

Nancy was very thoughtful that evening, and shortly after the supper dishes had been washed she offered an excuse and went to her room. She had received a letter from her father that afternoon and now brought it out to read over again.

"I have been wondering what progress you have made with the coded telephone message," he had written. "I am sorry that I have not had time to help you, but doubt that I should be of much assistance in any case. I really believe you would do well to turn it over to an expert."

"Perhaps Dad is right," Nancy told herself with a sigh.

She took the coded message from her purse and worked over it for perhaps two hours. At the end of that time she was no nearer the solution than before, and was forced to the realization that she was only wasting time.

"How foolish I've been," she thought. "I shouldn't expect a person who knew nothing of law to win a case, and yet I'm trying to decipher a code which might baffle an expert.

"Time is precious just now, for if I delay I may lose my chance to spring the *coup de grace*. The thing to do is to turn this message over to a cryptographer. Tomorrow I'll drive to the city and see if I can find one. If I can't do better I can turn it over to the police!"

Relieved that she had reached a decision, Nancy carefully returned the paper to her purse, and went to bed.

Little did she know, as she fell into a sleep as peaceful as that of a child, that an adventure was waiting for her just around the corner!

CHAPTER XIV

An Accusation

"WHAT do you say to taking a little jaunt in the sedan?" Nancy proposed to her friends the following afternoon. "I feel as though I'd enjoy a ride and I have some business to transact in the city, so we can kill two birds with one stone."

"Lonesome for the skyscrapers already?" George bantered.

It was a delightful day for driving and the girls were really looking for an excuse to take to the road. George and Bess climbed into the back seat of the sedan and soon they were off. They stopped briefly at the first town, where Millie left a can of cream and then, their duties over, settled themselves for an enjoyable ride.

"This is great," commented Bess.

The heavy car rolled smoothly over the hills, and the scenery seemed even prettier than when the girls had viewed it on their first trip over the road. For some time Nancy drove on steadily.

"Isn't your gasoline tank nearly empty?"
Millie asked presently.

Nancy nodded.

"I'm glad you reminded me. Watch for a
station and we'll stop."

A mile farther down the road Millie sighted
one, and then looked surprised.

"Why, it's the same place where we stopped
for luncheon the day we were on our way to
Red Gate Farm!" she cried.

Nancy turned in at the gravel driveway, but
as two other cars were ahead of her she drew
up some distance from the gasoline pump.

"How about an ice cream soda?" she asked.
"I'll stand treat."

George, Bess, and Millie enthusiastically
agreed to the suggestion and followed Nancy
and Millie into the lunch room. They took seats
at one of the tables, but though they were the
only customers no one came to wait upon them.
From an inner room, evidently used as an office,
they could hear excited voices.

"Something appears to be wrong," Nancy
said to her companions.

In a few minutes two men who looked like
detectives came out of the office in company
with the filling station attendant and the woman
who served as cashier of the lunch room. The
woman was talking excitedly.

"We found the twenty dollar bill in the cash

register at the end of the day. It looked like any other money, and we didn't suspect anything was wrong until Joe took the day's receipts to the bank. They refused to accept the twenty, saying it was counterfeit!"

One of the men picked up the bill which the woman had placed upon the counter as an exhibit. He glanced at it and then tossed it contemptuously aside.

"Sure, it's counterfeit, all right. There's been a lot of that kind of money passed around here lately. We'll get that gang but it will take time. They're a clever outfit."

"We were cheated out of twenty dollars," the woman declared vehemently. "It isn't fair to hard working people like Joe and me. It looks as though investigators should be able to do something about it!"

"We'll do all we can," was the slightly impatient answer, "but unless you know who it was that passed the bad money I don't see what we'll be able to do. As I said before, this gang is especially clever."

"It was a girl that gave me the bill," the woman insisted. "There were several of them in the party. I'd recognize her in a minute."

Though Nancy and her chums could not help overhearing the conversation, it did not once enter their heads that their party was the one under discussion. The woman had been so agitated with her troubles that she had not noticed the girls. After waiting nearly ten minutes George proposed that they leave.

"It's clear we'll not get any service until after those investigators leave," she said, "and if we're to reach the city and get back before dark, we must hurry."

Nancy arose with the others, though she was particularly interested in what the woman had been saying about counterfeiters, and would have liked to have heard more.

As the girls were crossing to the door, the woman took note of them for the first time. Her jaw dropped down and she stared hard, first at Nancy Drew, then at her three friends, and finally back at Nancy.

"That's the one! She's the very girl who gave me that counterfeit bill!"

Nancy and her companions halted as suddenly as though they were puppets operated by strings. They could not believe that they had heard aright. What happened next removed all doubt from their minds.

"Arrest that girl!" the woman screamed. "Don't let any of them get away—they're all in on it together!"

One of the detectives interposed himself between the girls and the door.

"Just a minute," he said cooly. "What's your hurry?"

"We're on our way to the city," Nancy returned, "and since there seemed little likelihood that we should ever be waited upon, we decided to leave."

"Not until you've answered a few questions," the man retorted grimly. He thrust the counterfeit bill rudely into her face. "Ever see that before?"

"How should I know?" Nancy demanded in exasperation. "It looks like any other twenty-dollar bill, though I just heard you say it was counterfeit!"

"She asked me to change it for her!" The woman broke in. "Isn't that so, Joe?"

"It sure is!" was the firm response. "She bought some gasoline, too!"

"You admit you've been here before?" one of the detectives demanded, addressing Nancy.

"Why, yes," Nancy admitted. She was somewhat confused by the sudden accusation and scarcely knew what to say. "But I deny that I passed a counterfeit bill!" she continued.

"Young girls don't usually go around cashing twenty-dollar bills to pay for ice cream sodas," the investigator said sternly.

"My father gave it to me because I was going on a vacation."

"A likely story!" the woman sneered.

"It's the truth!" George spoke up indignantly. "The idea of accusing my chum of passing bad money! It's ridiculous!"

"Ridiculous, is it?" the woman retorted angrily. "You'll sing a different tune when you land in jail!"

"Look here, you can't arrest us for something we didn't do!" Bess protested.

"Oh, I guess you did it, all right," one of the detectives returned. "At least, it won't hurt to take you into the city and let you spin your yarn to the higher-ups!"

"But you're arresting us upon flimsy evidence," Nancy cried indignantly. "I tell you we know nothing about the bill! Do you think we would come here this afternoon if we had tried to pawn off bad money?"

This question struck home and the two agents looked at each other somewhat doubtfully, and at Nancy with respect.

"I tell you she gave me that bill!" the woman cried. "She practically admitted it a minute ago."

"I admitted that I asked you to change a twenty-dollar bill," Nancy agreed, feeling that she had unwittingly placed herself in an awkward situation, "but when you say I gave you *that* bill you're taking a whole lot for granted."

"It was the only twenty which came in that day," the filling station owner declared.

"Why, that isn't true," Nancy corrected. "I distinctly remember that three men drove up in a big car and after you had filled their gasoline tank, one of the men who had a large roll of bills came in here."

"Do the rest of you swear to that?" the detective questioned Nancy's companions.

Bess, George and Millie looked rather blank and this was instantly counted against them.

"My friends were inside the lunch room at the time," Nancy explained.

"I do remember seeing a man come in," Bess declared after a moment, "but I didn't pay any particular attention to him."

"These girls are trying to work out an alibi for themselves," the woman who operated the lunch room broke in indignantly. "A gentleman did come in that same afternoon to buy some ginger ale but he didn't ask me to change any large bill for him."

"But the man used a bill in order to pay for his gasoline," Nancy insisted. She turned to the filling station attendant, suddenly recalling that he had taken the twenty-dollar bill into the lunch room himself to make change.

Before she could state this fact the man forestalled her.

"The next thing she'll be sayin' is that I changed the bill myself!"

"Well, didn't you?" Nancy demanded.

The attendant bristled.

"Guess I'd know a counterfeit bill if anyone tried to pass one off on me," he declared hotly.

Nancy realized that the man and his wife had no aversion to telling one falsehood after another. Probably they believed the girls guilty, and yet, unable to consider anything save their own loss, they were taking unfair methods to secure an arrest. Nancy could tell that the investigators were impressed with their story.

"If you arrest us, you'll find that you've made a silly mistake!" she said indignantly to the men. "I don't know who passed that counterfeit bill but I do know that those three men who stopped here looked like suspicious characters!"

"It doesn't do you any good to try to pass the buck," she was told. "Four birds in hand are worth a couple of dozen in the bush. You'll have to come along with us."

"We've told you the truth," Nancy insisted.

"That may be," was the even response, "but you'll have to prove your story."

"How can we prove that we didn't pass that bill?" Nancy demanded in exasperation. "It's our word against theirs!"

"You'll have to come along," one of the detectives repeated impatiently. "Better not
make trouble!"

In despair the four girls exchanged frightened glances. What were they to do? Millie,
Bess and George looked to Nancy, hoping that
she might save them, but Nancy was at her
wits' end.

"At least, permit my friends to return
home," she pleaded. "If anyone is at fault it
is I alone."

"You'll all have to go," was the grim response. "Come along! It won't do any good
to make trouble!"

The girls were grasped roughly by their arms
and pushed toward the door.

CHAPTER XV

A Friend in Need

THINGS looked very black indeed for Nancy and her friends. The investigators had discredited their story and now the girls were completely at a loss to know how to save themselves from this situation.

What should they do?

Unobserved by Nancy and her chums, an automobile had driven up and parked near the filling station. As the girls were forced to the door of the lunch room, a tall young man alighted and came that way. He halted abruptly as he saw the two detectives.

"Hello!" he exclaimed. "What's going on here, anyway? Why, you girls look as if you had lost your last friend!"

Nancy looked up and saw Mr. Auerbacher's son, Karl Jr., standing in the doorway. How he had happened to arrive at such a critical time she neither knew nor cared. The important thing was that he had driven up at the psychological moment and might be able to help them out of their present unfortunate predicament. She felt that she had never before been so glad to see anyone.

"Oh, Mr. Auerbacher," she cried joyfully. "I'm so glad you came! They're trying to arrest us!"

"What's this?" Karl Jr. demanded in astonishment. "You're joking!"

"It's no joke," Nancy returned earnestly. "We were out for a little ride this afternoon and happened to stop here for something to eat. When we started to leave they accused us of passing counterfeit money. The only basis they have for the accusation is that we stopped here once before, and I foolishly gave them a twenty-dollar bill."

"Look here," Karl Jr. said bluntly, turning to the two investigators. "You can't hold these girls. Release them at once!"

"Who are you?" one of the agents questioned curtly. "What right have you to interfere?"

"My name is Karl Auerbacher, and these girls are my friends. As it happens, my father is living at Red Gate Farm in Round Valley. I was on my way there when I thought I'd stop here for a bite to eat. Lucky I did, too!"

"Sorry if these girls are friends of yours," one of the men said in a tone which indicated that he was not particularly disturbed, "but they'll have to go with us."

"I don't know yet what this mixup is all

about," Karl Jr. returned, "but if you're accusing these girls of deliberately trying to pawn off counterfeit money, you're crazy!"

"You're willing to vouch for their honesty?" he was asked.

"Most assuredly. This young lady," Mr. Auerbacher indicated Millie, "is the granddaughter of Mrs. Burd, the owner of Red Gate Farm." He turned to Nancy. "And this is Miss Drew. No doubt you have heard of her father, the famous lawyer. If you haven't, you soon will!"

"Not Carson Drew of River Heights?"

"Yes," Karl Jr. drawled, "and unless you anticipate difficulties of an embarrassing nature I'd advise you not to arrest either his daughter or her friends."

"Why didn't you tell us who you were?" Nancy was asked.

"You didn't give me a chance to tell you anything!" Nancy retorted. "You seemed to want to believe what these other persons said."

"I still think they're guilty," the woman who operated the lunch room declared angrily. "If they didn't give me that twenty-dollar bill, who did?"

"I'm sure it was one of those men who drove up in that fine automobile," Nancy insisted. "They flashed a huge roll of bills. The filling station attendant saw the money. Didn't you?"

"Well, I do recollect that three sporty men stopped for gasoline," the attendant admitted with a change of attitude. "It slipped my mind until just now."

"Don't you remember that one of the men gave you a twenty-dollar bill and you came in here to change it for him?" Nancy demanded sharply.

"I did change a bill," the man admitted reluctantly, "but I thought it was a ten."

"You see," Karl Jr. broke in, "the charge against the girls amounts to that!" He snapped his fingers contemptuously.

The two agents looked at each other in perplexity. In truth, they did not know whom to believe, but the fact that Nancy was the daughter of a famous lawyer made it wise for them to act with the utmost caution.

"We may have made a mistake," they admitted with a show of good grace. "We had to take the word of the owner and his wife. You see, a clever counterfeiting gang has been operating in this part of the state, and we know several women are mixed up in the affair. In the hope of breaking up the outfit we've been tracing every clue."

"Well, take care that you don't hook into any more false ones," Karl Jr. returned grimly. He turned to the girls. "Let's get out of here."

The girls hurriedly left the lunch room in
company with Mr. Auerbacher. The detectives
leisurely followed them outside, observing their
actions.

As Nancy was about to step into the sedan,
she thought of something which she wished to
report to the investigators. It occurred to her
that by some remote chance they might be interested in the coded message which she had
brought with her.

She was firmly convinced that the three men
who had stopped at the filling station were the
ones who had passed the counterfeit twenty-
dollar bill, undoubtedly with deliberate intent.

Though she did not have positive proof that
the men were affiliated with the mysterious
"Al" of Room 305, intuition told her that there
was a definite connection.

"I may as well give the coded message to
these agents," Nancy told herself. "They
might be able to decipher it and perhaps learn
what sort of business is being conducted in that
office. It will save me a trip to the hot city."

Accordingly, she moved over to where the
two agents were leaning against the lunch room
door, and quickly told them about the strange
reception she and Millie had received when
they had visited the office in Riverside Heights
in answer to the advertisement.

"The man in charge of the place was so secretive about his business that I thought something was amiss," she explained. "Then I learned that Yvonne Wong was there——"

"You know her, then?" one of the agents questioned.

"No, I saw her name in the paper," Nancy returned. "I had met her by accident when she was selling perfume in an Oriental shop——"

"Yes, we know all about that," she was told.

"Yvonne is no friend of mine," Nancy went on hastily, feeling that these men had misunderstood her. "I was merely curious to know who had secured the position my friend wanted."

The officials exchanged quick glances which Nancy could not understand. Feeling that they considered her information trivial, she brought out the coded message.

"I took this down while in the office," she told them. "It is part of a message which was telephoned in. I'm sure it must be a code but I haven't deciphered it."

She was rewarded by seeing the two men look startled. One of them took the piece of paper and scanned it with interest.

"It does look like a code," he said, and then asked Nancy several questions about how she had obtained the message.

She answered frankly, for she had nothing to conceal. She did not mention her suspicions regarding the cave at Red Gate Farm, for she intended to investigate that angle herself. Then, too, the matter was a delicate one. She must do nothing which might result in unfavorable publicity for Mrs. Burd or her granddaughter Millie.

"We'll investigate this clue all right," the two detectives assured her. "Just leave it to us!"

Nancy thanked the men, though she felt that they might well thank her. She was not altogether certain that she had done the right thing in giving them the paper. Perhaps they would only pigeonhole the message, and that would be the end of it. They had seemed interested, and yet there was something strange about their attitude.

"We'll never get to the city unless we hurry," Bess protested to Nancy when she returned to the car. "All this silly fuss has delayed us dreadfully. I don't know what would have happened if Mr. Auerbacher hadn't appeared at the psychological moment."

"Let's turn back to Red Gate with him," Nancy proposed. "I've decided not to go to the city after all."

The girls already had thanked their new friend for the timely rescue from the stern hand of the law, but they continued to shower gratitude upon him until he was embarrassed.

"Shall we be on our way?" he asked. "I

want to reach Red Gate Farm in time to have a
good visit with my father and still return to the
city this evening.''

Nancy was forced to pull up to the gasoline
pump. By the time she was ready to take the
road, Karl Jr. was a considerable distance
ahead of them.

"Step on it!" George advised. "We don't
want him to get too far along.''

"We may get into more trouble," Bess re-
flected gloomily.

The big sedan rapidly gathered speed, and
under Nancy's skillful handling fairly shot
down the road.

The two detectives watched the car disappear
around a bend.

"Looks like she's mighty anxious to get
away," one of them remarked. "Think her
story was the straight goods?"

"Hard to tell," was the response. "You can
tell she's a clever girl—but the clever ones need
the most watching!"

The other nodded.

"It won't do any harm to see what we can
do with the message she turned over to us, but
at the same time it may pay us to keep an eye
on her! You can't tell who the criminals are
these days, although I can't say these girls
looked anything like crooks.''

"Right!" his companion agreed. "Even if

she is the daughter of a famous lawyer, she may be mixed up in the affair. We'll follow at a safe distance and see if she really goes to Red Gate Farm.''

With that, the two agents sprang into their high-powered car and took to the highway.

CHAPTER XVI

UNAWARE that they were being followed,
Nancy and her chums continued toward Red
Gate Farm. After a few miles they succeeded
in catching up with Karl Auerbacher, but did
not find it easy to keep close behind his automobile, for he was a fast driver.

Even though Nancy drove swiftly, the detectives' car always managed to keep her sedan in
sight. Had the girls chanced to look back they
would have realized at once that they were being
followed. As it was, they were so overwrought
discussing the treatment they had received at
the lunch room that it did not occur to them
to turn around.

"It was lucky for us that Mr. Auerbacher
happened along when he did," Bess declared.
"Imagine spending the night in jail!"

"They couldn't have held us," Nancy said.
"They didn't have the slightest evidence
against us!"

"Just the same we'd have had trouble prov-
ing our innocence," Millie commented. "And

our names might have been printed in the newspapers.''

"Yes, it would have been embarrassing all around,'' Nancy agreed. "You know, I couldn't figure out those detectives. Even after Mr. Auerbacher told them who we were, they acted strangely.''

"They must have believed our story or they wouldn't have permitted us to leave,'' Millie commented.

"Yes,'' Nancy said slowly, "apparently they did, but when I talked with them alone, I couldn't decide what they were thinking.''

"You shouldn't expect to be a mind reader along with all your other accomplishments,'' George laughed. "By the way, what was that secret conference about, anyway?''

"It wasn't particularly secret,'' Nancy returned. "I merely told the agents that I thought it might pay them to investigate that office we visited—Room 305.''

"You think they're engaged in counterfeiting there?'' Millie gasped.

"I don't know what to think,'' Nancy admitted with a troubled frown. "I feel convinced that some unlawful business is going on. Since Yvonne Wong is working there I'm inclined to believe that the syndicate which was dissolved by government order has been reorganized and is doing business again.''

"But it takes special machinery for counterfeiting," Millie protested. "There wasn't anything like that there."

"I know," Nancy admitted. "Counterfeiting is probably a wild guess. I confess I never even thought of it until those agents brought up the subject. If it isn't counterfeiting, an investigation may uncover what is wrong in that office."

It was fairly late in the afternoon when the two automobiles turned in at Red Gate Farm. Karl Jr. greeted his father, tactfully avoiding any mention of what had occurred at the lunch room. The girls told the story themselves, stressing the part played by their handsome rescuer. While they were talking in the front garden, a low-swung car moved slowly past the farmhouse.

"I wonder who that was?" Mrs. Burd remarked, half to herself. "There were two men in the car and they were looking this way as if they knew someone. Did you notice, Millie?"

"No, I didn't, Granny."

It developed that Mrs. Burd was the only one who had seen the car, and so the subject was dropped. Karl Jr. proved such a charming entertainer that by dinner time the girls had forgotten counterfeiters, syndicates and even the Nature cult on the hillside. Everyone was sorry to see him leave later in the evening.

"I wish I could stay," he said regretfully, permitting his eyes to rest especially long on Nancy, "but I must get back to the city to-night. I'll try to run down again in a few days to see Father."

"You can't tell me 'Father' is the only attraction at Red Gate Farm," George said teasingly after Karl Jr. had gone. "He has his eye on Nancy!"

"Silly!" Nancy laughed.

"He scarcely took his eye off you all evening," George insisted. "You made quite a hit this afternoon when you played the rôle of the rescued heroine."

"Oh, go climb a sour apple tree!" Nancy retorted.

Bess joined in the teasing until poor Nancy blushed.

"Karl Jr. wouldn't be so bad," George went on, "but imagine having old Mr. Auerbacher for a father-in-law!"

"You do the imagining," Nancy said lightly. "I'm going to bed."

The girls were abroad early the next morning, for they had gradually accustomed themselves to farm hours. They had planned to go berrying, but at breakfast Mrs. Burd disappointed them by saying to Millie:

"I'm afraid you'll not be able to go with the girls, Millie. I must have some groceries from town, and Reuben is too busy to drive in.''

"Can't you wait until afternoon?" Millie asked. "The girls won't know where to find the best berry patches without me. Must you have them this morning?"

"I'm afraid I can't wait," her grandmother answered regretfully. "I must have some of the things before dinner. Mrs. Salisbury will complain if I don't give her a cup of cocoa as usual. I should have given you my shopping list yesterday, but you were gone before I knew it."

"Let me go to town for you, Mrs. Burd," Nancy proposed. "Honestly, I'd rather do it than go berrying and I know Millie wants to go with the girls."

"I shouldn't think of troubling you," Mrs. Burd protested.

Not until she saw that Nancy really wanted to do the errand, did she consent to the arrangement.

Soon after breakfast Nancy took the shopping list and drove away in the sedan. She had gone perhaps a mile when she sighted an old lady hurrying along the side of the country road.

The old woman limped slightly and appeared to be excited about something.

"I'll offer her a ride," Nancy decided. "She seems to be in a dreadful hurry."

Accordingly, as she drew nearer, she halted the car and called:

"May I give you a lift to town?"

The woman glanced up, startled. Nancy saw her face for the first time. It was the old lady from Black Snake Colony whom she had aided several days before on the river trail! What she was doing so far from her camp Nancy did not know, but she determined to make the best of the opportunity which had presented itself.

CHAPTER XVII

AN IMPORTANT LETTER

"PLEASE get in," Nancy urged, as the woman hesitated. "I'm sure your foot must be paining you considerably. I notice that you are still limping."

"Thanks," the woman returned gratefully, hobbling over to the car door which Nancy held open for her. "I am in a great hurry to get to town."

Before stepping into the automobile she looked quickly over her shoulder as though fearing that someone might observe her action.

She sighed in relief as she settled back against the cushions, looking very white and exhausted.

"Surely you weren't intending to walk all the way to town?" Nancy asked in a friendly, conversational tone.

The woman nodded.

"I had to get there."

"But aren't the members of your Colony permitted to use any of the cars I've seen around the camp?" Nancy questioned, watching her companion particularly closely, and hoping that she might tactfully glean some information.

"We aren't allowed much freedom," was the short answer.

"You shouldn't be walking on that foot yet," Nancy protested. "You're apt to injure your ankle permanently."

"It's nearly well now," the woman told her, avoiding Nancy's eyes. "They didn't know at the camp that I was going to town. I—I left in a hurry."

Again she cast an anxious glance over her shoulder. It occurred to Nancy that the woman was afraid of being followed.

Was she running away, or had she in some way incurred the wrath of the leaders?

When Nancy had encountered the woman in the woods, she had considered her as old, but now she saw that it was worry which had lined her face. She was really not more than middle-aged, but undoubtedly it was a hard life that had left its marks.

Nancy longed to ask her companion a number of personal questions and to learn more of the strange cult with which she was affiliated, but the woman's aloof attitude warned her that such inquiries would be ignored or evaded.

Deciding upon an entirely different course, she pretended not to pay particular attention to her companion. For some time they drove along in silence. Nancy could see that the woman was gradually relaxing and losing her fear.

"Am I going too fast for you?" she inquired, when she felt that the time was right to launch the conversation.

"Oh, no," the woman returned quickly. "You can't go too fast for me. I'm in a big hurry to get to town." She hesitated, and then added, "I have an important letter to mail."

"Why don't you drop it in one of the roadside mail boxes," Nancy suggested casually. "The rural carrier will pick it up and save you a long trip to town."

"I want to get it off this morning if I possibly can."

"I'll be going to the post office myself," Nancy next said, purposely drawing the woman out. "If you wish, I'll be glad to mail it for you."

"Thank you kindly," the woman mumbled, "but I think I'd best mail it myself. I—I'll feel better about it if I do."

As Nancy did not reply, she said:

"I don't mean to be ungrateful for all you've done—really I don't. It's only that I don't want to get you into trouble."

"How could I get into trouble by helping you?" Nancy asked with a smile.

"You don't understand," her companion assured her nervously, "and as I said before, there are things I can't explain. The leaders of the Colony will be very angry with me if they find I have left camp even for a few hours."

"I can't understand why you tolerate such rigid supervision," Nancy said impatiently. "Why, the leaders of the cult must treat the members as prisoners!"

"It's an unhappy life," the woman confessed.

"Then why don't you run away?"

The question startled the woman. She glanced sharply at Nancy, then as quickly looked away.

"I would if I dared," she said at length.

"Why don't you dare?" Nancy challenged. "I'll help you."

"No, you mustn't get mixed up in this," was the firm answer. "The time isn't ripe yet. Perhaps later I can get away."

"I don't see what anyone can do to you if you decide to leave the Colony," Nancy went on. "Surely you're a free agent."

"Not any more," her companion returned sadly. "I'm in it too deep now. I'll have to go on until fate helps me."

"I wouldn't wait for fate," Nancy advised bluntly. "Let me help you—today!"

"No, I'll not drag you into it," the woman responded. "You don't know what you'd be getting into if you helped me. Why, if they even learn that you've aided me in mailing this letter——''

Nancy saw the woman shudder. For one fleeting instant she, too, felt afraid—afraid of something which she could not define, an unseen hand, the power of which she could not fathom.

She realized that the woman was trying to warn her of danger. Nancy knew that the wise thing to do was to forget all about the Nature cult and the strange things which apparently went on at the hillside cave.

Yet, though intuition told her that she had better heed the warning, she knew that she could never turn back, for now she felt herself to be on the verge of discovering an important secret.

If her courage did not fail, the next ceremonial meeting would see the mystery solved!

CHAPTER XVIII

HELPFUL GOSSIP

NANCY's companion obviously was relieved when the sedan rounded a bend and brought them within sight of the town.

"If you'll just drop me off at the post office I'll be much obliged," the woman said to her.

"May I not take you back with me?" Nancy asked. "I'll be returning in less than an hour. I haven't much to do."

"No, I'll not trouble you any more. I'll walk back."

Nancy saw that it was useless to protest and so allowed the matter to rest. She could not understand why the woman was so afraid that they would be seen together.

She made no comment, however.

She let her passenger off at the post office and then continued down Main Street, until she came to the grocery store. While she was waiting for her order to be filled, two women entered the store. They were talking earnestly together, and did not pay particular attention to Nancy. Nancy, in turn, did not notice them, until one began to speak on a subject which startled her.

"It beats all the way those people carry on," she heard one of the women say. "You would think Mrs. Burd would turn them off!"

Instantly Nancy was listening.

"I suppose she needs the money," came the response, "but someone should speak to her about it. The idea of those folks capering around in bed clothes! They must be crazy!"

"That's just what I think!" the other woman answered. "If I lived near that farm I wouldn't feel safe!"

"And I hear they're to have another one of their pow-wows tonight! It's to be some special mystic ceremony. Whoever heard of such nonsense?"

As a clerk came to wait upon them the two women dropped the conversation. Nancy, however, had heard enough to be convinced that they had been speaking of the Nature cult. They were blaming Mrs. Burd, too, for something which was not her fault.

"Things are becoming serious," Nancy told herself. "I must do something quick, or everyone around here will be criticising poor Mrs. Burd."

If the two country women were correct, another big ceremonial would be held that very night on the hillside of Red Gate Farm! That meant that Nancy's opportunity had arrived. In the face of the warnings she had received, did she dare take it?

Nancy scarcely gave the question second thought, so eager was she for the adventure.

"I'll not drag Millie and the others into it, though," she decided. "If anything should go wrong, I'd feel responsible. One person in trouble is enough."

As soon as she had finished buying the groceries, Nancy went directly to the dry goods store. There she purchased a bolt of white cloth and various sewing articles.

"I'll need to be economical for the remainder of the week," she told herself as she ruefully surveyed the contents of her purse, "but if this venture turns out the way I anticipate, it will be worth the expense!"

Loading everything into the car, she started back toward Red Gate Farm. Enroute, she maintained a sharp watch for the woman from Black Snake Colony, but she was nowhere along the road.

"She must have taken to the fields," Nancy decided. "Doubtless she is afraid of being seen by me or anyone else."

Millie, Bess and George were just returning from the woods with their pails filled with berries, when Nancy drove into the barn yard. They helped her carry the packages into the house. George glanced curiously at the fat one which Nancy kept tucked under her arm, but did not venture a question as Mr. Auerbacher and Mrs. Salisbury were within hearing distance.

Immediately after the midday meal Bess proposed a game of horseshoe. All except Nancy agreed enthusiastically.

"I believe I'll go to my room," she told them. "I have a little work to do. I'll join you a little later."

"Oh, let it go," George pleaded. "It makes uneven sides unless you play."

"This is important work I have to do," Nancy laughed. "Get Rube to play. He throws a wicked shoe!"

The hired man was waiting for an invitation, and so the girls reluctantly left Nancy to her own devices.

"I can't for the life of me understand why gals want to sulk in their rooms," Mr. Auerbacher grumbled. "Better forget your troubles and go out and have a good time."

"I haven't any troubles," Nancy called back over her shoulder as she mounted the stairs, "and furthermore, I have something more vital than sulking to do!"

She was no longer annoyed at Mr. Auerbacher's sallies or Mrs. Salisbury's advice, for she had learned to pay slight heed. No doubt

their advice was well meant, but certainly it
was not in keeping with modern times.

Nancy carefully closed the bedroom door behind her. Then she unwrapped the bolt of
cloth and brought out scissors, needle, thread
and thimble.

"Now for it!" she chuckled.

She whistled a gay little tune as she cut out
the costume which was to serve as an entering wedge to the Nature cult ceremonial. She
snipped, and fitted, and stitched, and was so
absorbed in her work that she entirely lost
track of the time.

She was startled by a loud pounding on the
door. Before she could answer, her chums
burst into the room.

"Nancy Drew, what are you doing?" Bess
demanded suspiciously. "You're up to something or you wouldn't stay cooped up here on
such a lovely day."

George seized the white garment in Nancy's
lap and held it up.

"What's this?"

"I've decided to join the Black Snake Colony," Nancy laughed. "They're having a
ceremonial tonight. I heard about it while I
was in town."

"And you didn't tell us a thing about it!"
Bess accused. "Why, you mean thing!"

"I intended to tell you about it before I went

off tonight," Nancy defended herself, "but I've been thinking the matter over and it seems to me this may be a dangerous mission. I don't want you girls mixed up in it."

"Well, you needn't think we'll stay at home," George declared. "If there's danger or fun to be had, we want some of it!"

"You don't care if we tag along, do you?" Millie asked timidly.

"Why, of course not," Nancy returned promptly. "In fact, I rather dread going alone. I just didn't want to let you in for anything dangerous."

"Then forget it," George advised bluntly. "I'm inclined to believe those hillside folks are harmless, anyway!"

Nancy made no response, but she felt otherwise.

"What shall the rest of us do for costumes?" Bess asked.

"There's enough material for everyone," Nancy told her. "It's getting late, though, and if you really intend to go, you'll have to get busy! The costume is easy to make but the headdress takes time. So get busy. A prize to the first one finished!"

Without delay, the girls set to work on the cloth, and for the next two hours they worked furiously. It was tedious work sewing the long seams by hand, but they were afraid to use the sewing machine downstairs, knowing that it would lead to questions.

At last the costumes were finished. The girls could not control their laughter as they tried them on.

"You certainly look like a spook!" George told Nancy. "Oh, I'm so afraid of you." She danced around the room in pretended fear.

"Do you think I'll pass?"

"Under the moon, they'll not be able to tell you from a full-fledged member of the cult," Bess declared. "Let's see you go through the mystic rites."

To the delight of her friends, Nancy danced about the room, waving her arms wildly and emitting weird moans.

"Millie!" a voice called up the stairway. "Dinner is ready!"

Startled, the girls scrambled out of the white robes and hastily folded them away in the bottom of a bureau drawer. They tried to compose their faces as they hurried downstairs but merely succeeded in looking guilty.

" 'Pears to me you girls spent a long time locked up in your rooms," Mrs. Salisbury sniffed suspiciously.

Nancy and her chums smiled pleasantly but offered no explanation. They were so excited over the prospective adventure that they did not do justice to the excellent meal Mrs. Burd

had prepared. Almost before the others had
finished, they whisked the plates into the
kitchen and had them washed in record time.

"I wish it would hurry and get dark,"
George fretted.

"Do you suppose Mrs. Salisbury and Mr.
Auerbacher intend to sit out there on the porch
all night?" Bess whispered impatiently.
"They'll be sure to see us leave and know
what's up."

"We can slip out the back way," Millie suggested. "It's farther that way, but we'll not
be seen."

"Did you tell your grandmother what we
were going to do?" Nancy asked.

"I told her that we might do a little investigating when the Colony held their next ceremonial. I didn't tell her we were going tonight,
for I was afraid she would worry."

As the shadows deepened the girls became
more impatient to be off. Several times they
glanced toward the hillside, but there was no
sign of activity.

"Are you certain tonight is the night?"
George asked Nancy somewhat doubtfully.

"All I know is what I heard those two women
say, whom I saw in town."

"It's early yet," Millie declared. "They
never hold the ceremonial until after it gets
very dark."

Presently the girls went to their rooms. Collecting their regalia they slipped down the stairs, and since Mr. Auerbacher and Mrs. Salisbury were arguing violently on the front porch, went out the back way.

Giving the house a wide berth, they entered the woods. It was already dark beneath the dense canopy of trees, and Bess gripped Nancy's hand. Millie was familiar with every path and led the way toward the hillside.

A weird cry broke the stillness of the night. Involuntarily the girls halted and moved closer together.

"What—was—that?" Bess chattered.

"Only some wild animal," Nancy returned firmly.

That afternoon it had been fun to think of investigating the hillside cave, but it was a different matter in the gloomy woods. Nancy sensed that the morale of the group was weakening. A word from her would send them all flying back toward the farmhouse and assured safety.

"Come on, girls," she urged, conscious of the tremble in her voice," we must hurry or we'll miss the excitement!"

CHAPTER XIX

SIGNIFICANT DEVELOPMENTS

LED by Nancy, the girls hurried on through the dark timber. The moon was rising, and ghostly rays of light filtered through gaps in the foliage overhead. A faint breeze stirred the leaves, and to the girls it seemed that they were whispering menacingly.

Presently the adventurers reached the river trail and followed it.

"We must be careful now," Nancy warned in a low voice. "We're drawing near the camp. The cult may have a lookout stationed to see that no one interferes during the night ceremony!"

"That's right," commented Millie.

"I almost wish I hadn't come," Bess murmured nervously. "I had no idea it would be as dark as this."

"It will be lighter when the moon rises higher," Nancy told her. "Still, if you want to turn back——"

"No, I'm going on if the rest of you are!"

"There's nothing to be afraid of!" George

158

scoffed. "No use getting one's self worked up. Nobody is going to scare me!"

"I'm not so sure," Nancy murmured under her breath.

She realized, more than did her friends, the serious nature of their undertaking. While Millie, Bess and George were inclined to believe that the members of the Colony were harmless folk, she was firmly convinced that they were unscrupulous persons. She was of the opinion that the mystic rites held on the hillside were nothing but a sham, no doubt employed to throw the country people off the track. It was to prove this theory that she had proposed the daring investigation. That there was danger to be met was a foregone conclusion, since the woman she had aided had warned her to keep away from there.

Fortunately for Nancy's purpose, the hillside was covered with large rocks and scattered trees which would afford temporary hiding-places. As the girls stole cautiously up the steep path, there was no sign of activity about the camp.

"It doesn't look as though there's anything doing tonight," George said in disappointment.

"We're probably early," Nancy reminded her. "Let's find hiding-places now and quietly wait. We'll have to scatter about."

They separated, George and Bess crouching

down behind a huge rock, and Millie and Nancy secreting themselves behind a dense growth of shrubs and tall grass.

For nearly ten minutes the girls waited impatiently.

Then, unexpectedly, Nancy heard an unusual sound.

"What was that?" she whispered tensely to Millie who crouched at her side.

"It sounded like an automobile!" Millie returned excitedly.

"There's more than one!"

"They must be coming up through the pasture," Millie said, listening intently.

An instant later the two girls saw the headlights of three automobiles.

"Strange they keep their lights on," Millie whispered.

Nancy did not consider it odd, for it fitted in with her theory that the persons in the cars intended their actions to be observed.

"Look!" Millie plucked her by the sleeve. "The cult members are coming out of their tents now!"

Nancy had already observed the white-robed figures walking slowly toward the three automobiles which had parked near the brow of the hill. She counted only six persons in costumes.

"I thought the Colony wasn't a very large

one," she told herself. "Apparently they import nearly all of their members for the secret ceremonial!"

The girls were too far away to hear what was being said, but they could see distinctly. They watched as a group of men and women, twelve in number, stepped from the automobiles. Nancy was too far away to recognize any of the faces.

The newcomers quickly donned white garments and headgear similar to that which Nancy and her friends had with them, and joined the members of the Colony. Horns tooted and whistles were blown.

"That's to call attention to what they are doing," Nancy whispered. "I'm sure they want the country people to see their ceremony —probably it's a means of frightening the neighbors away."

The cult members soon began capering and dancing about in the moonlight, and Nancy felt that the time was now ripe for the daring attempt to join the group. Before she could communicate this thought to Millie, there was a slight stir in the bushes directly behind her.

Involuntarily Nancy jumped, for she fully expected to see one of the Colony members pounce down upon her.

It was George and Bess.

"Isn't it about time to start something?" the former asked in a whisper. "They seem to be busy with their own affairs now."

"Yes," Nancy agreed, "we must slip into our robes as quickly as we can."

Being well hidden by the rocks and bushes, the girls donned their costumes and pulled the headgear over their faces.

"Wait!" Nancy warned, placing a detaining hand upon George, who was impatient to be away, "we can't blunder now or the game will be up! We must slip quietly into the circle one at a time."

"My knees are shaking now," Bess admitted. "I don't know how I'll be able to dance."

"Stay here if you like," Nancy told her. "I think we should leave someone to keep guard. No telling what might happen, and it will be just as well to have someone stationed here. Then, if things go wrong, she can go for help."

"Not a bad idea," George approved. "You stay, Bess."

"I should say not! Much as I hate the thought of going into that cave, I'd prefer it to staying here alone!"

"Someone should stay," Nancy said. "Shall we draw for it?"

"I'll stay," Millie offered. "I know the

way back through the woods better than you girls do.''

"Come on," George pleaded, plucking at Nancy's sleeve. "If we don't hurry, we'll be too late!''

"Good luck!" Millie whispered as the girls crept away.

Inch by inch, they made their way up the hill. At length they crouched behind a clump of bushes not a dozen feet from where the cult members were moving about.

The girls dared not whisper, for the slightest sound might give them away, but Nancy indicated that she would make the first attempt to break into the group. Bess and George nodded in agreement. Now that the actual moment for courage had arrived, even George was losing her enthusiasm for the venture.

The slightest mistake would surely mean detection!

Nancy felt her heart beating more rapidly than usual, but she was not afraid. Waiting patiently until the right moment came, she suddenly slipped out among the white-robed figures, and instantly began waving her arms and making grotesque motions.

Her first nervousness over, she was elated to find that her entry into the group had not been observed. If only George and Bess were as successful! She was not much worried about

George, but Bess was frightened and might blunder.

Nancy watched her disguised companions, and quickly saw that she would have no trouble in following the motions. She did not even need to pay strict attention, for each person was doing something different, apparently made up on the spur of the moment.

"So far, so good," Nancy told herself in great elation.

Satisfied now that her own position was temporarily secure, she tried to help her chums. Deliberately moving over toward the shrubs behind which George and Bess were hiding, she shielded them from the view of the cult members, all the time continuing her grotesque motions.

George realized at once what she was endeavoring to do and made the most of the opportunity. Choosing her time, she slipped out and joined the group on the hillside. Bess was more timid. Several times at the critical moment she hesitated, and lost her chance for the time being.

George and Nancy were about to despair, when Bess summoned all her courage and made the plunge.

"Keep close together," Nancy warned in an undertone when Bess had successfully joined the group. "If we once lose each other, it's goodbye!"

By this time the girls had made up their minds that there was nothing mystic about the queer rites of the Black Snake Colony. They felt very silly indeed as they pranced about. Then, too, disguised persons on all sides of them were making crude remarks which assured the girls that the cult members did not take the ceremony seriously.

"This ought to give the country yokels an eyeful!" Nancy heard one man mutter.

"How much longer do we have to do this?" another grumbled. "I'm getting sick of flapping my arms around like a windmill!"

"This cult idea was all foolishness anyway!" still another offered.

"Foolishness, is it?" someone caught him up. Nancy thought she recognized the voice but could not be certain. "Let me tell you a girl was prowling around here only a few days ago! I guess the Chief knew his business when he thought up this cult idea, all right."

From the snatches of conversation Nancy and her friends knew that some underhanded business was being conducted. What it was, they were determined to learn before the night was finished!

"Well, I guess we've had enough of this!" a

loud voice presently announced. Nancy decided that the man must be one of the leaders. "We may as well go into the cave and get down to business!"

George was just wondering what the girls better do, when Bess clutched Nancy's hand and whispered nervously:

"Dare we enter?"

"I shall," Nancy returned quietly. "We haven't learned anything yet."

Nevertheless, as she saw the white-robed figures marching single file toward the entrance of the cavern, she, too, had misgivings.

CHAPTER XX

INSIDE THE CAVE

As NANCY and her chums followed the members of the Nature cult toward the entrance of the cave, it occurred to them that they might be walking into a trap. Once inside, there could be no retreat.

"Keep close behind me," Nancy warned her companions in a whisper. "Whatever happens, we mustn't get separated!"

As they approached the mouth of the opening, following close behind the others, Nancy saw a tall figure, robed in white, standing guard. Her heart nearly failed her as she realized that each person, in filing past, was uttering some password.

"We're finished now," she thought. "I wonder what will happen to us."

It was too late to turn back. The three girls could do nothing but hope that in some way they might get past the stalwart guard. Just how that was to be done did not occur to any of them.

Nancy kept close to the person just ahead

of her, and as he muttered the password she managed to catch it.

"Kamar!"

When Nancy's turn came to pass the guard, she spoke the word clearly. As she had anticipated, George and Bess heard, and taking their cue from her they repeated the countersign. The sentry did not give them a second glance, yet the girls breathed easier when they were safely through the entrance.

They descended into a cold, damp tunnel. Someone was carrying a torch at the head of the procession, but Nancy and her friends, who were near the end of the line, were in semidarkness.

"What do you suppose we're getting into?" George muttered.

Nancy did not reply, but gave her chum a sharp nudge as a warning that she was to be silent. She realized how precarious was their position, for escape was now cut off. George was still considering the affair as a lark, forgetting the danger.

A moment later Bess tripped over some object in the path and would have fallen, had not Nancy clutched her by the arm. They descended farther underground, and then, unexpectedly, stepped into a dimly-lighted chamber.

The members of the cult sat down on the

floor, and the girls followed their example. As they waited for everyone to arrive, they became aware of a peculiar, yet rather pleasing odor. Nancy looked quickly about her to see if an incense-burner had been lighted.

Suddenly it dawned upon her that it was perfume! The same scent which had attracted her interest on a number of occasions! What could be its strange significance?

As one of the white-robed figures moved past her a moment later, she definitely located the source of the perfume. Evidently the individual who used the queer Oriental scent was the leader, for his bearing was confident and assured. This belief was confirmed when, after everyone had entered the chamber, the man threw off his headgear and glanced over the group appraisingly.

Nancy momentarily was stunned. She recognized the man but she did not know his name. She had first seen him that day at the filling station, and had every reason to believe that he had been involved in the affair of the counterfeit twenty-dollar bill. His companions had at that time addressed him as Maurice.

"Everyone here?" he demanded gruffly.

He counted the group, and again Nancy and her chums held their breath, fearful lest they be detected. Apparently some of the members of the Colony were missing, for the leader did not notice that three new recruits had been added to his organization.

"We may as well get down to business," the leader announced. "Sniggs, have you anything to report?"

At the question one of the disguised persons stood up and threw off his mask. Again Nancy was startled.

It was no other than the man she had seen in Room 305!

"Al Sniggs," she turned over reflectively in her mind. "Where have I heard that name before? I'm sure I've seen it in a newspaper or somewhere."

"What's on your mind, Sniggs?" the leader demanded. "Anything gone wrong at your office?"

"Not yet, Chief," was the muttered reply, "but yesterday I saw a bird hangin' around the building—looked like a plain-clothes to me. I don't want you to think I'm turnin' chicken-hearted, but if you ask me, I'd say it's about time to blow. This game won't last forever, you know."

"I'll do the thinking for this outfit," was the scathing retort. "We'll stay here another week and then we'll pick a new location. What makes you think the coppers are wise?"

"Well, they may have got wise to the fact that we're using Yvonne again——"

"That's right!" a shrill, angry voice interrupted. "Blame me! Every time somebody gets nervous, you bring me into it!"

Nancy could scarcely restrain herself. She had been right about Yvonne! The girl was mixed up in some underhanded deal.

"If only they'll go on," she thought hopefully, "and tell enough to implicate themselves! So far, I can't be certain what it's all about, although I have a sneaking suspicion!"

"You deserve blame," Al Sniggs retorted irritably. "First, you didn't have any more sense than to sell a bottle of that perfume to perfect strangers——"

"I told you I couldn't help myself!" Yvonne defended. "Those girls practically took it away from me. Anyway, I don't see what harm it did. They were only a bunch of high school girls."

"No," was the sarcastic rejoinder, "you're so simple-minded you wouldn't see that it might land us in jail! When Pete was on the train coming here he noticed the scent and thought one of the girls was the Chief's agent! Lucky for all of us, he saw his mistake before he'd spilled anything!"

The leader, whom Nancy was later to know

by the name of Maurice Hale, had become impatient at the argument.

"Enough of this! It's not getting us anywhere! Sniggs, I placed Yvonne in your office and she'll stay there as long as I say. I'm satisfied with her work. Get me?"

Sniggs nodded sullenly.

Nancy had been studying the leader intently and by this time was convinced that he was far more clever and intelligent than his subordinates. She had grasped the situation instantly. Al Sniggs was right-hand man to the Chief, but he resented his superior's favoritism for Yvonne Wong. The organization was a large one, of that she was certain, but it remained for her to learn what dishonest business was being conducted. If only she might discover that, she could slip away and bring the authorities!

"Another thing," Al Sniggs continued, addressing the leader, "we'd better make up a new code. It's safer."

"All right," was the response. "I'll work one out for you in a day or two."

He called upon another member of the organization for a report.

Being satisfied, he passed on to a swarthy member for an account.

"The distributing department is gettin' along

swell," was the gruff reply. "Not a question asked so far."

"Good!" the leader exclaimed, rubbing his thin hands. "Now, if you'll follow me to the work room, I'll dole out the money for the next week."

Nancy and her friends could not have retreated had they wished, and certainly they had no desire to leave the cave before they had learned everything. Boldly they followed the others into an adjoining chamber which was brilliantly lighted.

Prepared as they were for the unexpected, the girls were taken completely back at the sight which greeted their eyes!

CHAPTER XXI

COUNTERFEITERS!

NANCY's first impression upon entering was that the chamber appeared to be a cross between a printing shop and a United States mint.

Hand presses were standing about and several engraved plates had been left on a table. Various chemicals and inks were in evidence. Neat stacks of paper money lined the wall and other bills were scattered carelessly about on the floor. Never in all her life had Nancy Drew beheld so much money!

The room was cluttered with it. Twenty-dollar bills appeared to be everywhere. Money, still damp, was drying on tables. Nancy observed at once that all of the bills were of the twenty-dollar denomination.

At last she had the answer to the many questions which had been troubling her! She had learned the secret of the cave! The Nature cult was but a sham organization, its so-called mystic rites used only as a cloak to hide the work of a clever band of counterfeiters! It occurred

174

to her that Black Snake Colony was a fitting name.

Nancy had considered such a possibility before, but not very seriously. She had guessed from the beginning that Yvonne Wong was a suspicious character and that her connection with the firm in Room 305 would bear investigation. However, it had been only a guess that there was any connection between the city office and the organization which passed itself off as a Nature cult.

She understood now why Yvonne had been reluctant to sell her the Oriental perfume. Evidently it was used exclusively by the Chief of the counterfeiters, or on rare occasions by his agents. The members of the syndicate were familiar with the scent and regarded it as a sign that the person who was permitted to use it was in the favor of the Chief.

"No wonder that man on the train thought I was a member of the gang," Nancy told herself. "Naturally, seeing me again, he would be particularly suspicious and think I was an under-cover agent."

Now that the object of her investigation had been accomplished, she was eager to steal away as quickly as possible and bring back the authorities.

Nancy turned to communicate her intention to her chums. A slight tug at their robes was all that was necessary to make them understand, but to put the plan into operation was another matter.

The girls attempted to edge toward the chamber entrance by degrees, but Al Sniggs stood barring the door. For the time being escape was out of the question. They must bide their time!

As long as the members of the organization remained masked, the girls knew that they would be comparatively safe, but already several persons had stripped off their robes. Every minute that escape was delayed, the danger of detection increased.

Since it was impossible to slip away, Nancy made careful note of her surroundings and tried to stamp faces upon her mind. Save for Yvonne, the leader Al Sniggs, and the man she had seen on the train, all were strangers. Six persons besides her chums and herself remained masked.

As Nancy surveyed the elaborate equipment in the work-room, she realized that she was dealing with an unusually clever gang of counterfeiters. The engraved plate which had been copied from an actual United States government bill was a work of art. Probably the leader of the gang had at one time been noted as a skilled engraver, and had his talents been applied in an honest endeavor he might have won high acclaim. He had concentrated his efforts upon one denomination—the twenty-dollar bill. Nancy could not have told the counterfeit money from the genuine thing, for the picture of Jackson on the face, and the White House on the back, were correct in detail. Only the color and texture of the paper upon which the bills were printed appeared to be at fault.

The organization had chosen to operate in a farming community, thinking that it would be easier to hoodwink the country people, but had maintained a city office to facilitate distribution.

When Nancy thought that she would not be observed, she slyly picked up one of the bills and thrust it inside her robe. It would serve as evidence.

"We did a pretty fair week's work," Maurice Hale said gruffly as he sorted the bills into several large piles. "Another month like this and I'd say we'll all be on Easy Street."

"The racket won't last another month," Al Sniggs growled. "I tell you, the Federal Agents are getting wise."

"Bah!" was the contemptuous retort. "Let them be suspicious! They wouldn't think of this place in a thousand years!"

"No?" the guard sneered.

He went on deftly sorting the money. Nancy

and her friends watched him with increasing uneasiness. When the various members of the organization were called upon to accept their share of the counterfeit bills, they would doubtless remove their masks. Could the girls escape detection then?

Nancy realized that the situation was becoming increasingly serious. They must escape before the actual distribution of the money began. If only Al Sniggs would move away from the door!

One thought comforted Nancy. She had been wise enough to leave Millie on guard outside the cave. If worst came to worst and escape was cut off, Millie undoubtedly would become alarmed and hurry back to the farmhouse for help.

"We may have to make a dash for it!" Nancy warned George in a whisper. "If that man moves away from the door, be ready!"

Al Sniggs did not move, however, and it seemed to the girls that he was watching them. They wondered if their whispering had made him suspicious.

Bess trembled slightly, and moved nearer Nancy as though for protection.

Maurice Hale had finished sorting the money, and glancing over the assembly announced in a commanding tone:

"Well, those of you who haven't removed

your masks had better do it now. I want to be certain no one is here who shouldn't be!"

Nancy and her chums felt themselves go cold. They were trapped! There was nothing they could do now save make a wild dash for freedom and safety.

"Ready!" Nancy muttered under her breath.

Before the girls could put their ideas into action, they were startled by a loud commotion in the tunnel. An instant later the guard, who had been stationed at the entrance of the cave burst into the chamber, half dragging a young girl who fought viciously to free herself.

It was Millie!

CHAPTER XXII

Captured

Nancy's first impulse at seeing her friend was to dash forward and try to aid her, but instantly she realized the folly of such an act. George half started toward Millie, but Nancy restrained her.

"Wait!" she whispered tensely.

If the situation had been grave before, it was a hundred-fold more serious now, for with Millie captured there was no one to go for help. The girls must depend entirely upon themselves to escape from the cave. No one at the farmhouse knew where they were. To acknowledge Millie as a friend would be to throw away their last hope.

"Let me go!" Millie cried, struggling to free herself.

"Where did she come from?" Maurice Hale demanded unpleasantly.

"I saw her hiding out in the bushes," the guard informed him. "She was spying! But she got just a little too curious."

"Spying, eh?" A harsh expression settled

upon the leader's face. "Well, we know what
to do with snoopers!"

"It's all a mistake," Millie murmured, on
the verge of tears. "I didn't mean any harm.
I'm Mrs. Burd's granddaughter and I was
merely curious to know more about the cult."

Even as she spoke, Millie's eyes traveled
about the room, noting the stacks of money and
the queer printing-presses. She tried not to
show that she understood the significance, but
it was too late. The leader had observed her
startled expression.

"So?" he drawled unpleasantly. "This time
your curiosity has been the means of getting
you into serious trouble. You'll learn not to
meddle in affairs that don't concern you, by the
time we get through with you!" He turned
quickly to Sniggs. "Al, see that no one leaves
this room!"

"Yes, chief," the guard answered.

Nancy wondered what new calamity was
about to befall them. Her suspense was of
short duration, for Maurice Hale continued in
a cold, harsh voice:

"Just to make sure that other spies haven't
been stealing a march on us, I'll have everyone
remove his mask. Be quick about it, too!"

Nancy knew that their game was up. With
Al Sniggs blocking the door, flight was now impossible.

The others had already stripped off their headgear. Nancy saw revealed the woman whom she had aided in the woods and on the road, but the others were strangers.

As Nancy and her chums deliberately delayed removing their masks, matters were taken from their hands. One of the men stepped forward and snatched the white cloth from Nancy's face. George and Bess likewise were exposed.

For an instant there was a stunned silence— then angry cries arose from the members of the Black Snake Colony.

"They are the same ones who bought the Oriental perfume from me!" Yvonne Wong declared shrilly.

Al Sniggs pointed accusingly toward Nancy and Millie.

"Those two girls applied at our city office for a job!"

"It was only by accident," Millie protested. "I wanted to help my grandmother, and Nancy was just trying to assist me in finding the office——"

"Don't expect us to believe a trumped-up story like that," the leader said harshly. "We know all about why you were snooping around, and what's more, we know how to deal with such persons!"

"Oh, Maurice, please don't be too harsh with

the girls," a timid voice pleaded. "They didn't mean to do any harm."

Nancy turned quickly and saw that it was the woman she had helped in the woods who had spoken.

"Didn't mean any harm?" the leader drawled sarcastically. "Oh, no, of course not. They only wanted to land us all in jail! Not that you would care! If I had known what an old whiner you were, I'd never have married you! Now mind your own business and let me attend to this affair!"

In spite of the seriousness of her own situation, Nancy felt genuine pity for the woman. Doubtless, she was the wife of Maurice Hale and had been led into wrong-doing against her will. She had hated the life she had been forced to lead, but had evidently been unable to escape from it.

Frightened by the harsh words of her husband, the woman moved back into a far corner of the room. For one brief moment, Nancy had hoped that she might intercede in their behalf, but now she realized that the woman dared not say more.

"What'll we do with 'em?" the leader demanded. "We can't let them go. They know too much. It's dangerous!"

On all sides angry mutterings arose. Yvonne

Wong heartlessly proposed that the girls be tied up and left prisoners in the cave, but even the leader ruled down such a suggestion.

"We'll have to get them out of here," he said. "They'll be missed and a searching party might visit this cave. How about the shack at the river? It's in such a desolate spot no one would think of looking there until after——"

He did not finish the sentence, but from the sinister expression on his face Nancy and her friends guessed his meaning. He intended to lock them up in an isolated cabin and leave them without means of sustenance! In that way, their lips would be sealed.

A cry of anguish was wrung from the leader's wife. Rushing forward, she clutched her husband frantically by the arm.

"Oh, Maurice! You couldn't be that cruel!"

The leader flung her away from him with a force which sent her reeling against the wall. She uttered a little moan of pain and sank to the floor.

"Oh," screamed Bess.

Even the Cult members were startled.

"Be quiet!" ordered their chief.

The cruel action aroused Nancy. For an instant all eyes were centered upon the woman, and Nancy thought she saw her opportunity. She was quick to take advantage of it. She made a rush for the door.

Bess and George, equally alert, darted after her.

Al Sniggs, who stood guard in the doorway, was taken completely by surprise. He tried to stave off the attack, but the three girls were too strong for him. He did succeed in holding back George and Bess, but Nancy wriggled from his grasp. She hesitated as she saw that her friends had failed.

"Go on! Go on!" Bess screamed.

Nancy darted into the next room, while George and Bess struggled with their captor, endeavoring to block the door and give their friend more time.

"Stop that girl!" Maurice Hale shouted angrily. "If you let her get away, I'll——"

Nancy plunged into the tunnel and was swallowed up by darkness. She ran as one possessed, for she knew that the lives of her chums depended upon her ability to bring them help.

Her long white robe hindered her, but there was no time to tear it off. She held it high above her knees. Once she stumbled, but caught herself, and rushed on.

The tunnel seemed to have no end. Behind her, Nancy could hear pounding footsteps and angry shouts. She thought the men must be gaining. If only she could reach the mouth of the cave!

The tunnel wound in and out and several times Nancy brushed against the rough stone wall. So twisted was the trail that she began to fear she had taken a wrong turn.

Then, just as she was giving up hope, she beheld a dim light far ahead and knew that she must be nearing the mouth of the cave. No one appeared to be guarding the entrance. Her only chance!

In a moment more she had reached the open air.

"Saved!" Nancy breathed.

At that instant a dark figure loomed up from the grass. Nancy felt a heavy hand laid upon her shoulder!

CHAPTER XXIII

The Tables Turn

"Not so fast there, my girlie!" the man leered as he clutched Nancy firmly by the arm and whirled her about. "What's the big rush, anyway?"

Nancy, staring into his hard face, saw that it was the man whom she knew only by the name of "Hank." Frantically she struggled to free herself.

"Thought I'd seen you before!" the man muttered in satisfaction. "You're the girl I warned to keep away from here! This time, I take it, you're lookin' for something besides a straying cow!"

Nancy did not waste her breath in a reply. She could hear the footsteps coming nearer and knew that her game would be up in another instant. In desperation she tried to jerk herself free, but her captor only held her more tightly and laughed as she cried out in pain.

Nancy twisted and squirmed and kicked, but it availed her nothing. She only hurt herself by trying to get away. By the time the others

187

came running up, she had ceased to struggle and stood quietly awaiting what Fate had in store for her.

"Good thing you got her, Hank," the leader praised. "The little wild cat! We'll give her a double dose for this smart trick! No girl's going to put anything over on me."

At the entrance of the cave it was nearly as bright as day, for the full moon had risen high in the heavens. Maurice Hale glanced nervously about, as though fearing observation by unseen eyes.

"Get back inside," he sharply ordered his followers. "It's a clear night and some wise bird might see us without our costumes and wonder what is up. We must destroy the evidence as quickly as we can and clear out of this place at once!"

Even as the leader spoke, Nancy thought she heard a rustling in the nearby bushes. She told herself it was only the wind stirring the leaves. Rescue was out of the question, for no one knew that she and her friends had started out to visit the cave. How foolish they had been not to tell someone of their plans!

Nancy made no protest as she was dragged back into the cavern. She had abandoned all hope now of escape.

Bravely she tried to meet the eyes of her chums, for she saw that they were even more discouraged than she. Poor Bess was on the verge of tears.

"Cheer up, dear," she whispered encouragingly. "We'll find a way to escape yet."

Bess only shook her head. She was not to be deceived.

The members of the syndicate did not intend to give the girls a second opportunity to break away. At an order from the leader Al Sniggs found several pieces of rope and bound Nancy and her friends hand and foot. He seemed to take particular delight in tying Nancy's bonds cruelly tight.

"I guess that will hold you for a while," he grinned.

He would have stood gloating over the girls, had not Maurice Hale called him.

"Get to work!" the leader commanded impatiently. "Do you think we have the rest of the night? If we don't hurry up and get out of here, the cops are apt to be down on us! Don't know what this girl's done."

All went to work with a will, for the fear of the law had fallen upon everyone. With a sinking heart Nancy realized that the men intended to destroy the evidence.

"The machines that we can't take with us we'll wreck," Maurice Hale ordered. "If we save the plates we can start up again in a new locality. Get a move on!"

He stood over the men, driving them furiously. His wife had slumped down in a chair and had buried her face in her hands. She appeared crushed. Only once did she arouse herself.

"Maurice," she murmured brokenly, "why won't you give up this dreadful life—always running from the police? We were happy before you fell in with bad companions."

Her husband cut her short with a sarcastic reply. She did not venture to speak again, but sat hunched over, looking sorrowfully at the girls. Nancy knew that she wanted to help them, but did not have the courage.

The work of destroying the counterfeiting machinery went on, but several times Maurice Hale glanced impatiently at his watch.

"No use waiting until we're through here," he observed after a time. "We may as well get the prisoners out of here pronto. The sooner we're rid of them the safer I'll feel. Al, you may as well start on ahead with one of the automobiles. You know the way to the shack, don't you?"

"Sure," Al Sniggs agreed promptly.

"Then take Hank along to keep guard and get going!"

Nancy and her chums were jerked to their feet. The cords about their ankles were re-

moved to permit them to walk, but their arms
were kept tied securely behind them.

"Move along!" Al Sniggs ordered Nancy,
giving her a push forward and not doing it in a
gentle or polite manner.

Nancy took a few halting steps and then
paused as one turned to stone. Her eyes were
riveted upon the doorway. There stood Mr.
Auerbacher's son, Karl Jr.!

"Stand where you are!" he tersely ordered
the counterfeiters. "We have you covered!"

CHAPTER XXIV

A Timely Rescue

Karl Auerbacher was not alone. At his back were no less than seven Federal officers, each one armed.

So unexpected was their arrival, that the counterfeiters were stunned. For an instant no one moved. Then Maurice Hale with a cry of rage dived for the lamp which stood on a nearby table.

Before he could reach it, one of the officers grasped him roughly by the arm.

"None of that! We have you right this time, Hale. You'll not try any funny work with Uncle Sam again!"

The man cast a quick glance about the room and saw that escape was out of the question. He acknowledged defeat with an insolent smile.

"All right, you win this time."

His wife screamed.

His workers muttered.

He did not protest when handcuffs were placed upon his wrists. The other members of the syndicate submitted to the officers without trouble, although Yvonne Wong vehemently protested her innocence.

"I didn't know what it was all about until tonight," she cried angrily. "It isn't fair to arrest me! I've worked for Mr. Sniggs only a few days——"

"You'll have to think up a better yarn than that!" she was bluntly told. "Your name has been mixed up in underhanded deals before, but this is the first time we've been able to get any evidence against you."

As soon as the prisoners were well in hand, Karl Auerbacher rushed over to the girls and quickly freed their hands.

"Are you all right?" he asked anxiously. "The scoundrels didn't harm you?"

"We're all right," Nancy told him, "but if you hadn't arrived just when you did, it might have been a different story!"

She was on the verge of inquiring what had brought Mr. Auerbacher to the cave at the psychological moment, when she saw that the Federal officers were placing handcuffs upon the wrists of Maurice Hale's wife. Breaking away from her friends, she darted to the other side of the room.

"Oh, don't arrest her," Nancy pleaded. "She isn't like the rest. She tried to save us but they wouldn't listen to her."

"Sorry," the officials returned, "but we'll

have to take her along. If you want to intercede for her later, it may be we can have her
sentence lightened."

"She doesn't deserve a prison term," Nancy
insisted. "Her husband forced her to live the
life she did."

"You're sure of this?"

"Yes, my friends will tell you the same. We
overheard everything."

"We'll see what we can do for her," the
officers promised, and for the time being Nancy
had to be satisfied.

After the prisoners had been herded out of
the cave to the waiting government automobiles
and the plates used in the making of the
counterfeit bills had been confiscated, explana-
tions were in order.

"How did you know we had come here?"
Nancy asked Mr. Auerbacher.

"I didn't," he admitted. "In fact, my appearance on the scene was entirely luck. You
see, I was driving this way on business, and
since I was so near Red Gate Farm, I thought
I would drop in and see my father. A few
miles down the road I met these government
agents. They were searching for this hillside
cave and asked me if I knew where it was."

"You had heard me speak of it?" Nancy
asked him.

"Yes. I wasn't certain where it was, but I

had a general idea. When I learned that there was trouble in the air, I decided to come along. It certainly gave me a start when I saw you girls held prisoners!"

"It gave us one to see you, too!" George laughed. "A pleasant one, though. We had nearly given up hope."

"I never was so scared before in my life," sighed Bess.

"The detectives already knew that the counterfeiters were hiding in this cave," Mr. Auerbacher continued. "We had no idea how large the gang was, so we decided to approach cautiously.

"As it happened we were concealed in the bushes when Nancy made her break for freedom. It seemed unwise to strike then, for some of the members of the syndicate most likely would have managed to escape. We bided our time and cornered the entire gang inside the cave."

"I'm glad you didn't delay a minute longer," Bess declared. "I'm a nervous wreck as it is!"

"What I can't understand," Nancy said with a puzzled frown, "is how the detectives learned that the syndicate was operating in this place. Did you happen to hear them say?"

"I can't tell you that," Karl Auerbacher returned. "You'll have to ask them yourself."

Just then one of the officers came over to the

group, but before Nancy could ask a question he turned to her and extended his hand.

"Miss Drew," he said earnestly, "I want to thank you for your work which has resulted in the clearing up of one of the most baffling cases our department has ever had."

Nancy's eyes opened wide.

"I don't understand," she stammered. "What have I done?"

The agent smiled.

"Why, that coded telephone message you handed over at the roadside inn," the official returned. "Don't you remember?"

"Why, yes, now that you speak of it, I do, but I don't see——"

"It furnished just the clue we needed," she was informed. "To tell you the truth, our men didn't quite believe all of your story that day."

"I was afraid they didn't," Nancy smiled.

"I'm sorry to say that we were all sufficiently suspicious to watch your actions," the government man went on.

"At first little importance was attached to that scrap of paper, but more as a matter of form than anything else it was sent to the Bureau of Cryptography. This afternoon we received an answer from Washington."

"Did they succeed in deciphering the code?" Nancy demanded eagerly.

"Yes, it was a particularly difficult one.

That was why it took so long to get a reply."

"And what did the message say?"

"It was only a fragment, but the name Maurice Hale was mentioned. We've had dealings with him before, so it was easy to guess that he was engaged in his old business again."

"You learned about the cave through the message?" Nancy asked.

"Yes. I've forgotten the exact wording, but it stated that a special meeting was to be held at the hillside cave near Red Gate on this night. We rounded up our force and came as quickly as we could. So you see, Miss Drew, an apology is due you. We sincerely regret that you were subjected to embarrassing questions that day at the gas station."

"Oh, that's quite all right," Nancy said graciously. "I hold no grudge. It was a natural mistake. I'm glad that the mystery has been cleared up."

"This part of the country has been flooded with bad money the last few weeks," the official told her. "We were ready to jump at any clue, for we had been unable to make the slightest progress toward solving the mystery."

It was late when the four girls, escorted by Karl Auerbacher, left the cave. Nancy had promised that if necessary she would testify against the counterfeiters, but preferred that her name not be given publicity.

The girls had been so excited over the happenings ·of the night that it had not occurred to them that their long absence from the farm house might have occasioned alarm.

"The lights are all on," Millie observed as they approached the house. "Granny must have discovered that we skipped off. I do hope she hasn't been worrying!"

Before the girls reached the porch, Mrs. Burd came hurrying toward them. She clung tightly to Millie for an instant.

"I'm so glad you're back," she murmured in relief. "When I found you girls weren't in your rooms I didn't know what to make of it. You had said something about attending the next cult meeting, and then when we saw those folks parading on the hillside tonight, we were afraid you had gone there. Mrs. Salisbury said I had been very foolish not to put a stop to such nonsense. We could see part of the ceremony from the porch, but that was hours ago! When you didn't come back here, I became very much alarmed."

"I'm sorry," Millie said contritely. "We didn't intend to be gone so long. I would have told you we were going, only I thought you would worry more if you knew."

"The idea of gals running around the country at this hour!" Mrs. Salisbury sniffed from the porch. "This Nature cult is all foolishness, anyway."

"That's right," old Mr. Auerbacher agreed. "The less you meddle with their affairs the wiser you'll be!"

"You're wrong this time, Father," Karl Jr. announced, emerging from the shadow. "If the girls hadn't meddled a bit, those counterfeiters would have operated indefinitely."

"Counterfeiters!" the two boarders exclaimed together.

They were rather silent as Karl Jr. related all that had happened. In fact, it was not until the next day that Mrs. Salisbury recovered from the shock sufficiently to boast:

"Well, I always said the girls were up and coming!"

Old Mr. Auerbacher was very proud of the part his son had played in the affair, and from that day on never tired of telling the story over and over.

Mrs. Burd had nothing save praise to shower upon Nancy and her friends. However, the removal of the Black Snake Colony from her property left her with a serious financial problem.

"I'm glad they're gone," she said, "but I'll miss the money. I can't hope to rent the land again, for it isn't fertile enough for farming.

All this talk about counterfeiters is apt to give
Red Gate a bad name, too. I can't expect to
get any more boarders.''

"Publicity is a queer thing," Nancy said
thoughtfully. "Sometimes it works out to one's
advantage, and again it doesn't. It all depends
upon how it's managed.''

"Exactly," Karl Jr. agreed, watching her
with twinkling eyes. "Have you any suggestion as to how this particular case can be
handled successfully?''

Nancy shook her head ruefully. A moment
later, however, she sprang up from the porch,
her eyes dancing.

"Yes, I have! It just came to me then! I
have the most wonderful idea! We'll capitalize
that cavern and make enough money to lift a
dozen mortgages!''

CHAPTER XXV

NANCY'S ACCOMPLISHMENT

CARSON DREW halted his automobile at the side of the road, and with an amused smile studied a large signboard which read:

"Follow the arrow to Red Gate Farm! See the mysterious cavern used by counterfeiters! Admission twenty-five cents."

"That looks like Nancy's work," he chuckled. "I must be on the right road."

As he continued slowly in his car, he presently came to another sign, bolder than the first:

"Regain Health at Red Gate Farm. Boarders by Day or Week."

"Nancy certainly believes in that slogan, 'It pays to advertise,'" Mr. Drew thought. "I had no idea she was serious when she wrote that she intended to turn to advantage all that publicity Red Gate Farm received. It appears she's done it with a vengeance!"

It was Sunday afternoon and the traffic was unusually heavy. Carson Drew soon became suspicious that all of the cars were headed for the destination he had chosen. As he came within sight of the rambling old farmhouse, and saw dozens of automobiles parked along the roadside, he realized that his unexpected arrival at Red Gate might not be such an event after all.

He had not written Nancy that he was coming, for he had decided to make the trip on the spur of the moment. Recently, his daughter's letters had been most unsatisfactory. In substance she always wrote: "Having a wonderful time. Business is rushing here and Mrs. Burd and Millie still need me, so if you don't mind I'll stay another week."

Nancy's weeks had stretched on and on, until one day Mr. Drew decided that it was time he learned for himself just what was going on at Red Gate Farm.

He parked the automobile as near the house as he could and walked up the path. He noticed that the grounds were well kept and equipped with swings and huge umbrellas. A number of persons, evidently boarders, were loitering about the garden.

Before Carson Drew could reach the front door, it was flung open, and Nancy rushed to meet him.

"Dad!" she cried joyfully. "Why didn't you let me know you were coming?"

"Oh, I thought I'd surprise you all! So this

is what you call taking a quiet vacation on the farm! It looks more like a three-ring circus to me!"

"Don't you like it here?" Nancy demanded in disappointment.

"It's great!" her father returned quickly. "But the people! Where do they all come from, anyway?"

"Oh, everywhere," Nancy laughed. "We're running advertisements in several of the city papers now, you know."

"There's considerable I don't know," Mr. Drew replied with pretended severity. "Your letters have been brief and far between, to say the least."

"I'm dreadfully sorry," Nancy smiled. "You see, Dad, we've been very busy getting things in order. Mrs. Burd has ten summer boarders now and a long waiting list. We're building an additional wing to accommodate more guests." She indicated the west side of the building.

"It's always nice and quiet here except on Sundays," Nancy went on. "A great many persons drive out just to see the cave. We have a free picnic ground nearby and that helps attract tourists here."

"I see you have an eye for business all right," Mr. Drew chuckled. "Are you making much money?"

"Mrs. Burd has paid off the mortgage, and if things go on the way they have, she'll soon be on the road to prosperity," Nancy informed him proudly.

"Aren't you afraid the interest in the cave may die out? Sometimes publicity only results in a temporary flash of business."

"I know," Nancy admitted, "but we're not worrying about that. The real money comes in from the summer boarders, and Mrs. Burd is getting a wealthy class of people who like Red Gate Farm for itself. They came to see the cavern, and then remained because they liked the atmosphere."

Just then Bess, George and Millie came hurrying out of the farmhouse, and Nancy presented her father to Millie. She had changed a great deal in the last few weeks. The worried expression was gone from her face, and she was plumper and prettier.

Mrs. Burd, hearing the laughter, came out and she, too, met Nancy's father. Her eyes filled with tears as she told him all that the girls had done to help her.

"They've been wonderful," she declared simply. "I was completely discouraged before they came. Now everything is changed."

As Carson Drew was conducted from one place to another, he realized that Nancy and her friends had been responsible for many alterations and improvements. The farmhouse had been repainted, the interior had been refurnished in a more comfortable style, and a housekeeper had been installed to relieve Mrs. Burd of responsibility. As they walked about the grounds Nancy told her father of the difficulties which she had overcome.

"Mrs. Burd didn't believe in the idea at first, and Mrs. Salisbury gave her pessimistic advice. However, Millie was all for taking a chance, and she persuaded her grandmother to invest a little money in advertising. You can see for yourself that it has paid."

"I'm proud of you, Nancy," her father declared earnestly. "Not only for what you have done to help Millie and her grandmother, but on account of the way you rounded up that gang of counterfeiters."

"I didn't do it all by myself," Nancy laughed.

"No, but if you hadn't turned over that coded message to the authorities, things might have turned out differently. I couldn't have done better myself."

"You might have been minus a daughter," Nancy smiled. "If the government men hadn't arrived just when they did——"

"Let's not think about it," Mr. Drew said quickly. "I wish you didn't have such a penchant for getting into adventure and unearthing mysteries. Worrying about your safety is what keeps me so thin."

"I suppose I'm responsible for that tiny bald spot, too!" Nancy teased. "You really wouldn't want me to be sedate and prim, would you, Daddy?"

"No, I'm afraid I wouldn't," Mr. Drew admitted. "By the way, I think I have news for you, Nancy."

"What about?"

"The counterfeiters. Perhaps you read about it in this morning's paper."

Nancy shook her head.

"The papers always arrive a day late."

"The entire gang was sentenced to prison," her father returned. "Maurice Hale was given a particularly long term."

"And his wife?" Nancy asked. "I wanted to testify to her innocence but they didn't call upon me."

"Her sentence was suspended. I imagine she was let off because you intervened in her behalf."

After a bountiful dinner which was served on the porch, Nancy and her friends took Mr. Drew to the hillside cave. Reuben Snodgrass, looking most unlike himself in a new suit which was a trifle too tight, was in his element as he conducted groups of visitors through the cavern.

"I've collected fifteen dollars already to-day," he hailed Nancy as she came up with her friends. "This is a lot better than plowin' corn."

After they had all returned to the farmhouse, Mr. Drew broached the subject of Nancy's return to River Heights.

"There isn't much to do here any more," Nancy returned. "Everything is organized. I suppose I may as well go with you this afternoon. How about it, girls?"

"It's time we all went," George agreed. "My parents have threatened to come after me, but I've kept stalling them off."

Millie and her grandmother protested vigorously. When they saw that the girls were really serious about leaving, they tried to make them accept a share of the profits which had been made through the exploitation of the cave. Nancy and her chums would not listen to such a suggestion.

"It doesn't seem fair," Millie protested. "You've worked hard all summer and now you won't take a cent."

"If we've done anything, the fun we've had has more than repaid us," Nancy assured her. "It's been a wonderful summer. We've learned a lot about farming, too!"

At last, after Millie and her grandmother had promised to drive to River Heights as soon as they purchased their new coupé, and the girls in turn had assured their friends they would visit Red Gate Farm frequently, good-byes were reluctantly said.

A few minutes later, as the girls sped down the road in their car, they looked back—and kept on looking until Red Gate Farm faded away into the distance.

"Well, that's that," Bess said with a contented sigh. "Didn't I always say that adventure follows Nancy around?"

"You can't blame it on me this time," Nancy laughed, "for it all came from buying expensive perfume. Three dollars a bottle—but a bargain at any price!"

THE END

This Isn't All!

Would you like to know what became of the good friends you have made in this book?

Would you like to read other stories continuing their adventures and experiences, or other books quite as entertaining by the same author?

On the *reverse side* of the wrapper which comes with this book, you will find a wonderful list of stories which you can buy at the same store where you got this book.

Don't throw away the Wrapper

Use it as a handy catalog of the books you want some day to have. But in case you do mislay it, write to the Publishers for a complete catalog.

THE RIDDLE CLUB BOOKS
By ALICE DALE HARDY

**Individual Colored Wrappers. Attractively Illustrated.
Every Volume Complete in Itself.**

May be had wherever books are sold. Ask for Grosset & Dunlap's list

Here is as ingenious a series of books for little folks as
ever appeared since "Alice in Wonderland." The idea of
the Riddle Books is this, three girls and three boys decide to form a riddle club. Each book is full of the adventures of these youngsters, but as an added attraction
each book is filled with a lot of the best riddles you ever
heard.

THE RIDDLE CLUB AT HOME

How the members of the club fixed up a club room in the Larue Barn
and how they, later on, helped solve a most mysterious happening, and
how one of the members won a valuable prize, is told in a very pleasing
manner.

THE RIDDLE CLUB IN CAMP

Camping on the edge of a beautiful lake the club members fall in with a
mysterious old man known as the Hermit of Triangle Island. Nobody
knew his name or where he came from until the propounding of a riddle
solved this mystery.

THE RIDDLE CLUB THROUGH THE HOLIDAYS

This volume takes in a great number of winter sports, including skating,
sledding and building a huge snow man. It also tells how the club treas-
urer lost the dues entrusted to his care and what the melting of the great
snowman revealed.

THE RIDDLE CLUB AT SUNRISE BEACH.

Tells how the club journeyed to the seashore and how they kept up their
riddles and had good times. Once they got lost in a fog and marooned on
an island. Here they made a marvelous discovery.

THE RIDDLE CLUB AT SHADYBROOK

Many exciting adventures happen at the quaint old country place called
Shadybrook which the club visits.

THE RIDDLE CLUB AT ROCKY FALLS

How the club went exploring up the river and the adventures they had
in the woods, and what is more important and exciting, how they solved
the mystery of the deserted hotel.

GROSSET & DUNLAP, *Publishers,* NEW YORK

THE OUTDOOR GIRLS SERIES

By LAURA LEE HOPE

Author of "The Blythe Girls Books"

Every Volume Complete in Itself.

These are the adventures of a group of bright, fun-loving, up-to-date girls who have a common bond in their fondness for outdoor life, camping, travel and adventure. There is excitement and humor in these stories and girls will find in them the kind of pleasant associations that they seek to create among their own friends and chums.

THE OUTDOOR GIRLS OF DEEPDALE
THE OUTDOOR GIRLS AT RAINBOW LAKE
THE OUTDOOR GIRLS IN A MOTOR CAR
THE OUTDOOR GIRLS IN A WINTER CAMP
THE OUTDOOR GIRLS IN FLORIDA
THE OUTDOOR GIRLS AT OCEAN VIEW
THE OUTDOOR GIRLS IN ARMY SERVICE
THE OUTDOOR GIRLS ON PINE ISLAND
THE OUTDOOR GIRLS AT THE HOSTESS HOUSE
THE OUTDOOR GIRLS AT BLUFF POINT
THE OUTDOOR GIRLS AT WILD ROSE LODGE
THE OUTDOOR GIRLS IN THE SADDLE
THE OUTDOOR GIRLS AROUND THE CAMPFIRE
THE OUTDOOR GIRLS ON CAPE COD
THE OUTDOOR GIRLS AT FOAMING FALLS
THE OUTDOOR GIRLS ALONG THE COAST
THE OUTDOOR GIRLS AT SPRING HILL FARM
THE OUTDOOR GIRLS AT NEW MOON RANCH
THE OUTDOOR GIRLS ON A HIKE
THE OUTDOOR GIRLS ON A CANOE TRIP
THE OUTDOOR GIRLS AT CEDAR RIDGE

GROSSET & DUNLAP, Publishers, NEW YORK

THE BLYTHE GIRLS BOOKS

By LAURA LEE HOPE

Author of The Outdoor Girls Series

Illustrated by Thelma Gooch

The Blythe Girls, three in number, were left alone in New York City. Helen, who went in for art and music, kept the little flat uptown, while Margy, just out of business school, obtained a position as secretary and Rose, plain-spoken and business like, took what she called a "job" in a department store. The experiences of these girls make fascinating reading—life in the great metropolis is thrilling and full of strange adventures and surprises.

GROSSET & DUNLAP, *Publishers,* NEW YORK

FOR HER MAJESTY—THE GIRL OF TODAY

THE POLLY BREWSTER BOOKS

By Lillian Elizabeth Roy

Polly and Eleanor have many interesting adventures on their travels which take them to all corners of the globe.

POLLY OF PEBBLY PIT
POLLY AND ELEANOR
POLLY IN NEW YORK
POLLY AND HER FRIENDS ABROAD
POLLY'S BUSINESS VENTURE
POLLY'S SOUTHERN CRUISE

POLLY IN SOUTH AMERICA
POLLY IN THE SOUTH-WEST
POLLY IN ALASKA
POLLY IN THE ORIENT
POLLY IN EGYPT
POLLY'S NEW FRIEND
POLLY AND CAROLA
POLLY AND CAROLA AT RAVENSWOOD

THE GIRL SCOUTS BOOKS

By Lillian Elizabeth Roy

The fun of living in the woods, of learning woodcraft, of canoe trips, of venturing in the wilderness.

GIRL SCOUTS AT DANDELION CAMP
GIRL SCOUTS IN THE ADIRONDACKS
GIRL SCOUTS IN THE ROCKIES
GIRL SCOUTS IN ARIZONA AND NEW MEXICO
GIRL SCOUTS IN THE REDWOODS
GIRL SCOUTS IN THE MAGIC CITY
GIRL SCOUTS IN GLACIER PARK

GROSSET & DUNLAP, *Publishers,* NEW YORK

WESTERN STORIES FOR BOYS
By JAMES CODY FERRIS

**Individual Colored Wrappers and Illustrations by
WALTER S. ROGERS
Each Volume Complete in Itself.**

Thrilling tales of the great west, told primarily for boys but which will be read by all who love mystery, rapid action, and adventures in the great open spaces.

The Manly Boys, Roy and Teddy, are the sons of an old ranchman, the owner of many thousands of heads of cattle. The lads know how to ride, how to shoot, and how to take care of themselves under any and all circumstances.

The cowboys of the X Bar X Ranch are real cowboys, on the job when required, but full of fun and daring—a bunch any reader will be delighted to know.

THE X BAR X BOYS ON THE RANCH

THE X BAR X BOYS IN THUNDER CANYON

THE X BAR X BOYS ON WHIRLPOOL RIVER

THE X BAR X BOYS ON BIG BISON TRAIL

THE X BAR X BOYS AT THE ROUND-UP

THE X BAR X BOYS AT NUGGET CAMP

THE X BAR X BOYS AT RUSTLER'S GAP

THE X BAR X BOYS AT GRIZZLY PASS

THE X BAR X BOYS LOST IN THE ROCKIES

THE X BAR X BOYS RIDING FOR LIFE

GROSSET & DUNLAP, *Publishers,* NEW YORK

THE HARDY BOYS SERIES
By FRANKLIN W. DIXON

Illustrated. Every Volume Complete in Itself.

THE HARDY BOYS are sons of a celebrated American detective, and during vacations and their off time from school they help their father by hunting down clues themselves.

THE TOWER TREASURE
A dying criminal confessed that his loot had been secreted "in the tower." It remained for the Hardy Boys to make an astonishing discovery that cleared up the mystery.

THE HOUSE ON THE CLIFF
The house had been vacant and was supposed to be haunted. Mr. Hardy started to investigate—and disappeared! An odd tale, with plenty of excitement.

THE SECRET OF THE OLD MILL
Counterfeit money was in circulation, and the limit was reached when Mrs. Hardy took some from a stranger. A tale full of thrills.

THE MISSING CHUMS
Two of the Hardy Boys' chums take a motor trip down the coast. They disappear and are almost rescued by their friends when all are captured A thrilling story of adventure.

HUNTING FOR HIDDEN GOLD
Mr. Hardy is injured in tracing some stolen gold. A hunt by the boys leads to an abandoned mine, and there things start to happen. A western story all boys will enjoy.

THE SHORE ROAD MYSTERY
Automobiles were disappearing most mysteriously from the Shore Road, It remained for the Hardy Boys to solve the mystery.

THE SECRET OF THE CAVES
When the boys reached the caves they came unexpectedly upon a queer old hermit.

THE MYSTERY OF CABIN ISLAND
A story of queer adventures on a rockbound island.

THE GREAT AIRPORT MYSTERY
The Hardy Boys solve the mystery of the disappearance of some valuable mail.

WHAT HAPPENED AT MIDNIGHT
The boys follow a trail that ends in a strange and exciting situation.

GROSSET & DUNLAP, Publishers, NEW YORK

TED SCOTT FLYING STORIES
By FRANKLIN W. DIXON

Illustrated. Each Volume Complete in Itself.

No subject has so thoroughly caught the imagination of young America as aviation. This series has been inspired by recent daring feats of the air, and is dedicated to Lindbergh, Byrd, Chamberlin and other heroes of the skies.

OVER THE OCEAN TO PARIS;
or, Ted Scott's daring long distance flight.

RESCUED IN THE CLOUDS;
or, Ted Scott, Hero of the Air.

OVER THE ROCKIES WITH THE AIR MAIL;
or, Ted Scott, Lost in the Wilderness.

FIRST STOP HONOLULU;
or, Ted Scott over the Pacific.

THE SEARCH FOR THE LOST FLYERS;
or, Ted Scott, Over the West Indies.

SOUTH OF THE RIO GRANDE;
or, Ted Scott On a Secret Mission.

ACROSS THE PACIFIC;
or, Ted Scott's Hop to Australia.

THE LONE EAGLE OF THE BORDER;
or, Ted Scott and the Diamond Smugglers.

FLYING AGAINST TIME;
or, Breaking the Ocean to Ocean Record.

OVER THE JUNGLE TRAILS;
or, Ted Scott and the Missing Explorers.

LOST AT THE SOUTH POLE;
or, Ted Scott in Blizzard Land.

THROUGH THE AIR TO ALASKA;
or, Ted Scott's Search in Nugget Valley.

FLYING TO THE RESCUE;
or, Ted Scott and the Big Dirigible

DANGER TRAILS OF THE SKY;
or, Ted Scott's Great Mountain Climb,

GROSSET & DUNLAP, *Publishers,* **NEW YORK**